SCHOLA

Motivating
Math Homework

80 Reproducible Practice Pages That Reinforce Key Math Skills

New York • Toronto • London • Auckland • Sydney
Mexico City • New Delhi • Hong Kong • Buenos Aires

Teaching *Resources*

Previously published as part of the Ready-to-Go Reproducibles series (for Grades 4–5):
Fun 5-Minute Math Practice Pages © 2002 by Denise Kiernan;
Amazing Math Puzzles & Mazes © 1999 by Cindi Mitchell

Scholastic Inc. grants teachers permission to photocopy the designated reproducible pages from this book for classroom use. No other part of this publication may be reproduced in whole or in part, or stored in a retrieval system, or transmitted in any form or by any means, electronic, mechanical, photocopying, recording, or otherwise, without written permission of the publisher. For information regarding permission, write to Scholastic Inc., 557 Broadway, New York, NY 10012.

Editor: Mela Ottaiano
Cover design by Maria Lilja
Interior design by Keka Interactive
Illustrations by Mike Moran

ISBN-13: 978-0-545-23454-2
ISBN-10: 0-545-23454-9

Copyright © 2010 by Denise Kiernan; Cindi Mitchell
All rights reserved. Published by Scholastic Inc. Printed in the U.S.A.

1 2 3 4 5 6 7 8 9 10   40   16 15 14 13 12 11 10

Contents

Introduction 6

ADDITION & SUBTRACTION

Underwater Addition
Skill: Addition: 2-Digit With Regrouping 7

Slugger Stats
Skill: Subtraction: 2- & 3-Digit
With Regrouping 8

Addition & Subtraction Review
Skill: 2- & 3-Digit With Regrouping 9

MULTIPLICATION

Lost in the Museum
Skill: Prime Numbers 10

The Amazing Nut Hunt
Skill: Prime Numbers 11

Amaze Mr. Nelson!
Skill: Facts to 9 12

Pet Mystery
Skill: Facts to 9 13

Dizzy Dog Owners
Skill: Facts to 12 14

Crack the Safe
Skill: 2 Digits x 1 Digit 15

Multiplication on Ice
Skill: 2 Digits x 1 Digit 16

Multiplication Puzzler
Skill: 2 Digits x 1 Digit 17

Starry Skies
Skill: 2 Digits x 2 Digits 18

Brain Strain
Skill: 2 Digits x 2 Digits 19

More Doggone Riddles
Skill: 3 Digits x 1 Digit 20

Timothy the Tiger
Skill: 3 Digits x 2 Digits 21

Bacteria Breakout!
Skill: 3 Digits x 2 Digits 22

Tree's Company
Skill: 4 Digits x 1 Digit 23

DIVISION

Handy Robots
Skill: Dividing by 5 24

Matchmaker Math
Skill: Facts to 12 25

Division Banquet
Skill: Facts to 12 26

Inspector Widget
Skill: Facts to 12 27

Bargain Shopper
Skill: 1-Digit Divisor, Money 28

Teacher's Pet
Skill: 1-Digit Divisor 29

Dial an Answer
Skill: 1-Digit Divisor, Remainder 30

Hungry Astronaut
Skill: 1-Digit Divisor, Remainder 31

Chocolate-Chip Challenge
Skill: 1- & 2-Digit Divisors 32

Crisscross Number Puzzles
Skill: 1-Digit Divisor, 3-Digit Quotient 33

Professor Dee Vision
Skill: 2-Digit Divisor, 1- & 2-Digit Quotient ... 34

Pirate's Treasure
Skill: Multiplication & Division 35

Across the Great Divide
Skill: 2-Digit Divisor, Remainder 36

All Mixed Up
Skill: 2-Digit Divisor, 2-Digit Quotient,
Remainder 37

MIXED PRACTICE

Multiplication & Division Review
Skill: Multiplication & Division 38

Five & Dime & Quarter Store
Skill: Multiplication & Division, Money 39

Read All About It . . . Carefully!
Skill: Multiplication & Division,
Word Problems 40

ESTIMATION

Tic-Tac-Toe
Skill: Multiplication 41

Math Hunt
Skill: Division 42

Bees, Please!
Skill: Multiplication & Division 43

FRACTIONS

Fractions With Cheese
Skill: Naming Simple Fractions 44

Fractions Are a Breeze
Skill: Simplifying Fractions 45

Wake Up!
Skill: Simplifying Fractions 46

Skyscraping Fractions
Skill: Comparing & Ranking 47

Three Cheers for Fractions!
Skill: Comparing & Ranking 48

Egg Hunt
Skill: Identifying Equivalent Fractions 49

The Puzzle Factory Mystery
Skill: Addition With Like Denominators 50

Going Buggy
Skill: Addition With Unlike Denominators 51

Someone's in the Attic
Skill: Addition With Unlike Denominators 52

Curious Critter
Skill: Subtraction With Like Denominators 53

Underwater Mystery
Skill: Subtraction With Unlike Denominators .. 54

Fraction Factory
Skill: Mixed Review: Addition & Subtraction
With Unlike Denominators 55

The World's Biggest Ant
Skill: Identifying Equivalent Improper
Fractions & Mixed Numbers 56

Fishy Business
Skill: Identifying Equivalent Improper
Fractions & Mixed Numbers 57

DECIMALS

Decimal Construction
Skill: Place Value 58

Million Dollar Winner
Skill: Place Value 59

Mystery at the Abandoned Library
Skill: Comparing & Ranking 60

Line Up
Skill: Comparing & Ranking 61

Runaway Dogs
Skill: Rounding 62

Greedy Gretchen
Skill: Addition 63

Funny Bunnies
Skill: Addition 64

Shark Subtraction
Skill: Subtraction 65

Obstinate Oscar
Skill: Subtraction 66

Shopping Spree
Skill: Subtraction, Money 67

Discount Decimals
Skill: Addition & Subtraction, Money 68

Batter Up
Skill: Multiplying Decimals by Whole
Numbers, Money 69

Yikes! Moor Misstakes!
  Skill: Multiplying Decimals by Whole
  Numbers, Money 70

Clothes Crisis
  Skill: Multiplying Decimals 71

Calculator Math
  Skill: Multiplying & Dividing Decimals
  Using a Calculator 72

Measure Mania
  Skill: Converting Decimals to Fractions 73

AVERAGES & RATIOS

Not Your Average Track Meet
  Skill: Averages With Whole Numbers 74

On-Target Rounding
  Skill: Averages With Decimals 75

Ratio Picnic
  Skill: Ratios 76

GEOMETRY

Raising the Roof With Geometry
  Skill: Angles 77

Shape Sorter
  Skill: Shapes 78

MEASUREMENT

Fly the Coop
  Skill: Distance & Conversion 79

The Math Mower
  Skill: Area 80

Math Dives Deep
  Skill: Volume 81

Make "Time" for Math
  Skill: Working With Time 82

GRAPHING

Math on the Map
  Skill: Coordinate Grid 83

Graph Attack
  Skill: Circle Graph 84

Hop on this Number Line
  Skill: Line Graph 85

WORD PROBLEMS

Putting It All Together
  Skill: Mixed Skills 86

ANSWER KEY 87

Introduction

Welcome to *Motivating Math Homework*!

If you are in search of an easy and motivating way to help students build key math skills, you'll find exactly what you need in these 80 reproducible practice pages. This book is packed with super-fun activities designed to keep students engaged while they practice essential skills, including place value, addition, subtraction, and multiplication. Some of the pages feature mazes, riddles, connect-the-dots, and other fun formats. Not only do all of these homework sheets reinforce the skills students in grades 4–5 need to know, they also provide opportunities for them to sharpen their reasoning skills and problem-solving abilities.

Turn to the table of contents or the top of each page to find the skill you would like students to practice, make copies of the page, and distribute to students for homework. Because each page includes simple, clear directions, students can complete all of these activities independently. From time to time, however, you may also want to encourage them to work in pairs during class time as an effective way to share problem-solving strategies and communicate about mathematical ideas. While most of the activities simply require a pencil and eraser, occasionally, students will also need to use crayons or colored pencils. Finally, at the end of the book, you will find an answer key.

We hope you'll discover how useful and fun these activities are for students, and that they'll provide you with additional options throughout the school year. Invite students to put on their thinking caps, sharpen their pencils, pull out erasers, and get ready to have loads of fun—and learn along the way!

Addition: 2-Digit With Regrouping

Name_____ Date_____

Underwater Addition

Fill in the empty boxes so that all of the number sentences are true.

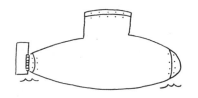

46	+	25	=	1.
		+		+
66	+	79	=	2.
		=		=
81	+	23	=	3.		4.		5.
		+						+
		49		29	=	6.		57
		=		+				=
7.				43	+	98	=	8.
				=
		9.	+	28	=	10.

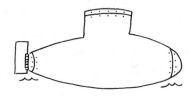

7

Subtraction: 2- & 3-Digit With Regrouping

Name _____ Date _____

Slugger Stats

Which slugger ends up hitting the most balls? The first number you see is the number of swings each batter took. The second number is the number of times the batter missed the ball. Your answer equals the number of hits made.

  1. 27
          − 8

  2. 172
          − 8

  3. 243
          −177

  4. 409
          − 98

  5. 32
          − 7

  6. 43
          −19

  7. 42
          −15

  8. 812
          −678

  9. 208
          − 19

 10. 75
          −66

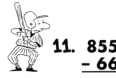 11. 855
          − 66

  12. 317
          −228

Circle the player who got the most hits.

How many hits did that batter get? _____

Did that batter take the most swings? _____

Addition & Subtraction: 2- & 3-Digit With Regrouping

Name_____ Date_____

Addition & Subtraction Review

Use all of your addition and subtraction skills to answer these questions as quickly—and correctly—as possible! Regroup if you have to.

1.   198
  + 27
	2. 70
	  − 39
		3. 609
		 − 80

4. 238 +542	5. 71 +39	6. 242 + 98
7. 28 −19	8. 422 + 87	9. 422 +89

10. 184
  −99
	11. 364
	  − 87
		12. 712
		  − 44

13. 803
  + 29
	14. 400
	  − 66
		15. 503
		  −165

Multiplication: Prime Numbers

Name_____ Date_____

Lost in the Museum

Andrew was lost in the art museum. When he found his way out, he discovered that he was missing nine tokens. Each token has a prime number on it, and when you add the numbers on the tokens, the total is 127. Can you find the nine tokens and put a circle around each of them?

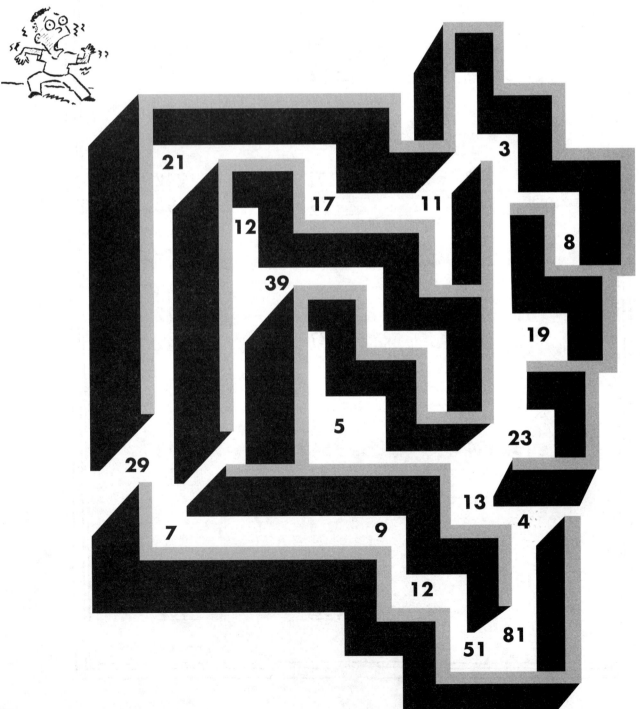

10

Multiplication: Prime Numbers

Name _____ Date _____

The Amazing Nut Hunt

Help the squirrel find its way to the nuts. Inside the star maze, its path can't cross any composite numbers. Draw a line to show the squirrel's path.

Multiplication: Facts to 9

Name_____ Date_____

Amaze Mr. Nelson!

Mr. Nelson has lost his grade book. Amaze him by finding it. Solve all of the multiplication problems. Find your way from the outside of the maze to the grade book without crossing any even products. Draw a line to show the path.

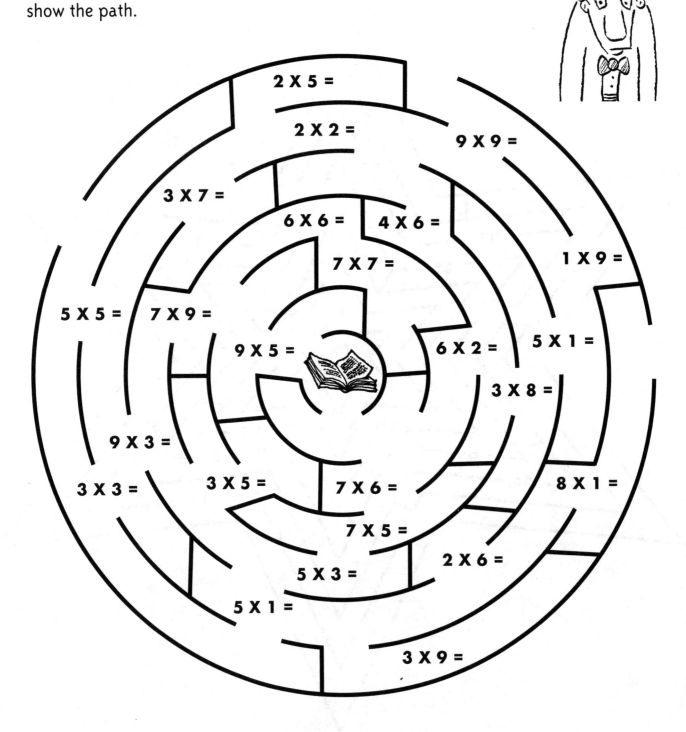

Name_____ Date_____

Multiplication: Facts to 9

Pet Mystery

Mrs. Doolittle bought a pet for our class. She's keeping it in a box until we can guess what it is. We need your help. Solve the multiplication problems. If the answer is even, shade the square. If your answers are correct, the shaded squares will tell us what kind of pet it is.

2 x 4	4 x 4	2 x 5	7 x 1	7 x 8	6 x 1	8 x 7	5 x 1	2 x 3	4 x 9	5 x 8
4 x 4	7 x 3	3 x 4	5 x 3	5 x 2	7 x 1	4 x 7	3 x 7	7 x 5	4 x 8	5 x 9
6 x 2	5 x 6	9 x 1	3 x 5	5 x 4	4 x 5	3 x 6	5 x 5	9 x 5	2 x 6	5 x 7
4 x 3	3 x 3	2 x 8	11 x 5	4 x 6	11 x 3	6 x 3	9 x 7	3 x 9	2 x 7	9 x 9
3 x 2	11 x 7	4 x 2	1 x 5	4 x 1	1 x 3	2 x 9	3 x 1	1 x 1	3 x 8	11 x 9

What is the pet? _____

Multiplication: Facts to 12

Name_____ Date_____

Dizzy Dog Owners

The dog owners at this show are seeing spots—on their Dalmatians, of course! They're so dizzy they've forgotten whose dog is whose. Match the dog to its owner by solving the multiplication problems. Then draw a line from the dog to the owner with the correct answer.

 **1.** 2 x 12 =

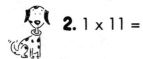 **2.** 1 x 11 =

 3. 5 x 6 =

 **4.** 4 x 8 =

 5. 9 x 7 =

 **6.** 8 x 8 =

 **7.** 9 x 3 =

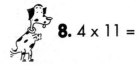 **8.** 4 x 11 =

 9. 3 x 4 =

 **10.** 6 x 7 =

Crack the Safe

Customers are getting mighty mad at Bank. They want their money. Unfortunately, Dennis the Duck doesn't remember how to turn the inside ring to open the safe. He knows that if the rings are lined up correctly, the factors in the inside ring multiplied by the factors in the middle ring equal the products in the outside ring. The two outer rings never move. Dennis left his calculator at home. Help him open the safe.

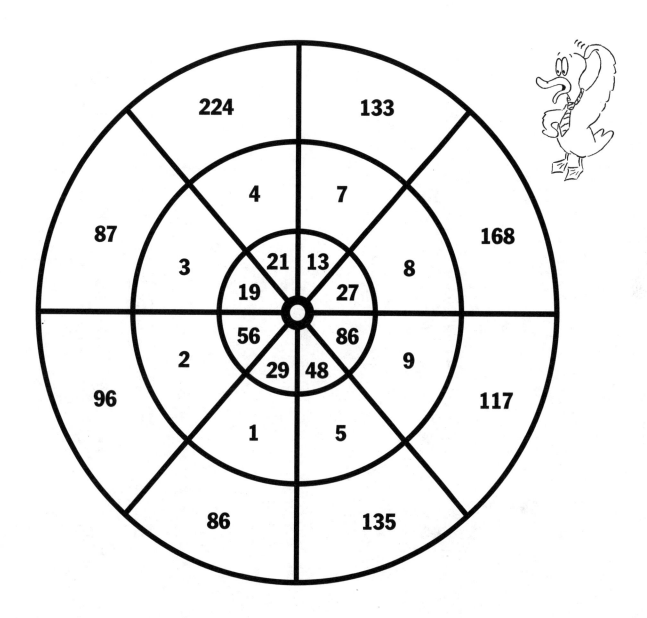

Solution: Dennis the Duck must turn the inside ring clockwise _____ places.

Multiplication: 2 digits x 1 digit

Name_____ Date_____

Multiplication on Ice

Who won the annual Multiplication on Ice competition? Solve the problems to find out. The skater with the highest number wins.

 1. 24
       x 2

 2. 32
       x 4

3. 20
    x 9

 4. 51
       x 9

5. 93
    x 3

 6. 63
       x 2

7. 82
    x 3

 8. 60
       x 8

9. 71
    x 9

 10. 14
        x 2

 11. 74
        x 2

 12. 52
        x 3

Who won? _____ Who came in second? _____

Who came in third? _____

16

Multiplication: 2 digits x 1 digit

Name_____ Date_____

Multiplication Puzzler

Each number below is contained inside a different shape.

EXAMPLE: The number 24 is inside a 24⌋ shape.

Write the correct number inside each shape in the box. Then solve each problem. Write your answer on the line. The answers are scrambled at the bottom of the page. A letter appears with each answer. Write the letter in the box next to your answer. You will have the solution to this riddle:

What was the hardest thing about learning to pole-vault?

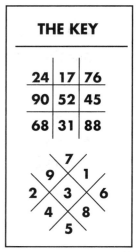

THE KEY

24	17	76
90	52	45
68	31	88

1. ⌋ × ⟨ = _____ ☐
2. ☐ × ⋁ = _____ ☐
3. ⌐ × ◇ = _____ ☐
4. ⌐ × ⟨ = _____ ☐
5. ⌈ × ⟨ = _____ ☐
6. ⌈ × ⟩ = _____ ☐
7. ⌊ × ⟩ = _____ ☐
8. ⌈ × ⋀ = _____ ☐
9. ⌊ × ⟩ = _____ ☐

THE DECODER	304 D	176 O	364 H	155 N	24 T
	204 E	540 G	153 U	360 R	

Multiplication: 2 digits x 2 digits

Name_____ Date_____

Starry Skies

A stargazer has to find the constellation with the most stars in it. To find out the number of stars in each silly constellation, do the multiplication problems.

1. 12
    x13

6. 83
    x19

2. 22
    x11

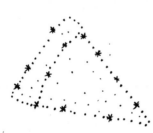

7. 94
    x13

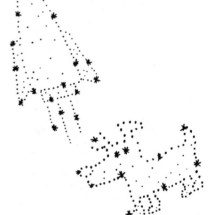

3. 18
    x14

8. 48
    x12

4. 13
    x12

9. 20
    x10

5. 28
    x27

10. 34
    x22

Which constellation has the most stars? _____

18

Multiplication: 2 digits x 2 digits

Name_____ Date_____

Brain Strain

Warning! This puzzle has been known to create serious brain strain. Approach with caution and be sure to use a pencil with a large eraser.

Find each product. Write the product in the puzzle. Each digit can occupy only one square in the puzzle. The first product has been done for you.

```
   14        29        21        56        77
 x 26      x 31      x 14      x 12      x 11
  364

   84        75        99        94        63
 x 81      x 75      x 99      x 92      x 22
```

Challenge: 595   582
              x 86   x 91

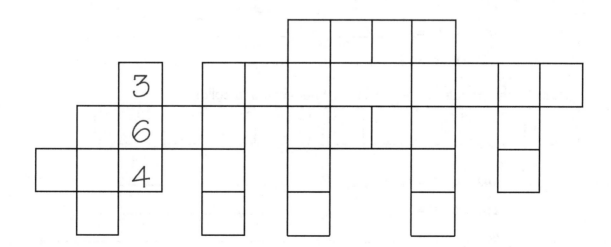

19

Multiplication: 3 digits x 1 digit

Name_____ Date_____

More Doggone Riddles

To find the answers to these tail-slapping riddles, solve the multiplication problems. Write your answer on the blank next to the problem. Then write one number, in order, on each line above a letter. Next write the letters in the boxes. Match the letters and numbers. The first problem is done for you.

156 X 5 = _780_   7 8 0
                            S K R

481 X 2 = _____
                           I E O

269 X 5 = _____
                           P O D L

What did the dog wear to the school dance?

1	2	3	4	5	6	7	8	9	0		
						S	K		R	T	

312 X 3 = _____
                        E U C

203 X 4 = _____
                        K P O

287 X 2 = _____
                        D A N

What kind of dessert did the dog refuse to eat?

1	2	3	4	5	6	7	8	9

139 X 7 = _____
                        T E G

103 X 8 = _____
                        I O G

123 X 5 = _____
                        N D O

What did the poodle say when she lost her diamond collar?

1	2	3	4	5	6	7	8	9

447 X 2 = _____
                        K E A

109 X 7 = _____
                        R A E

205 X 5 = _____
                        F T L M

Where did the dog refuse to go shopping?

1	2	3	4	5	6	7	8	9	0

Name_____ Date_____

Timothy the Tiger

Timothy the tiger is a weight lifter, and he loves to look at himself in the mirror. Only one of the reflections below is his real mirror image. Can you figure out which one it is and circle it? To check your answer, do the multiplication problems below each tiger. The product that matches the number under Timothy is his exact mirror image.

214	407	563	505	499
x 36	x 22	x 17	x 18	x 12

486	107	386	719	802
x 13	x 34	x 24	x 12	x 11

272	315	189	106	610
x 19	x 22	x 41	x 53	x 11

Multiplication: 3 digits x 2 digits

Name_____ Date_____

Bacteria Breakout!

These bacteria are math whizzes! They multiply . . . and multiply and multiply. Now they've broken out of their petri dishes and are on the run! Where are they off to? First, write the answer to each problem. Once you've finished, use your answers to solve the riddle below.

1. 387
    x 23
    _____
    (R)

2. 107
    x 55
    _____
    (Y)

3. 460
    x 12
    _____
    (M)

4. 776
    x 12
    _____
    (B)

5. 865
    x 11
    _____
    (N)

6. 331
    x 98
    _____
    (G)

7. 850
    x 30
    _____
    (E)

8. 100
    x 10
    _____
    (S)

9. 521
    x 64
    _____
    (A)

Q: Where do bacteria like to hide out?

A: $\overline{32{,}438}$ $\overline{25{,}500}$ $\overline{8{,}901}$ $\overline{5{,}520}$ $\overline{33{,}344}$ $\overline{9{,}515}$ $\overline{5{,}885}$

Multiplication: 4 digits x 1 digit

Name_____ Date_____

Tree's Company

Why do trees make bad party guests? You need to solve these multiplication problems to find out. First, write the answer to each problem. Once you've finished, use your answers to solve the riddle below.

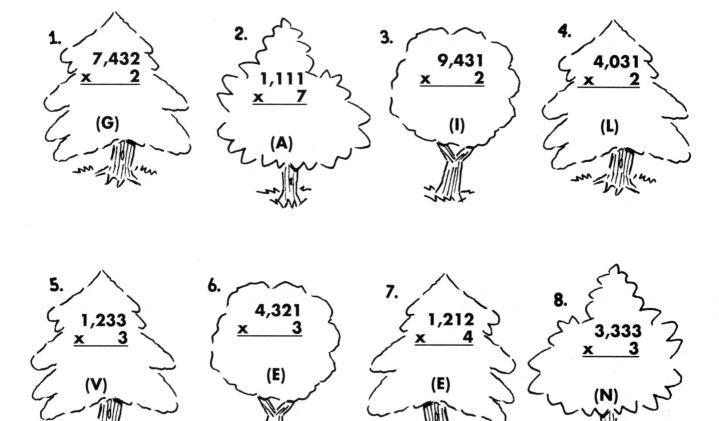

1. 7,432 × 2 (G)
2. 1,111 × 7 (A)
3. 9,431 × 2 (I)
4. 4,031 × 2 (L)
5. 1,233 × 3 (V)
6. 4,321 × 3 (E)
7. 1,212 × 4 (E)
8. 3,333 × 3 (N)

A: Because they're always

"_____ _____ _____ _____ _____ _____ _____"!
   8,062   4,848   7,777   3,699   18,862   9,999   14,864

23

Division: Dividing by 5

Name_____ Date_____

Handy Robots

Can you give these robots a "hand" finding new work gloves? First, look at the number of fingers each robot has. Then write a division problem that divides the number of fingers by 5, the number of fingers in a glove. Your answer will tell you how many gloves that robot needs.

 1. This robot has 10 fingers.

_____ ÷ _____ = _____

 2. This robot has 25 fingers.

_____ ÷ _____ = _____

 3. This robot has 20 fingers.

_____ ÷ _____ = _____

 **4.** This robot has 50 fingers.

_____ ÷ _____ = _____

 5. This robot has 45 fingers.

_____ ÷ _____ = _____

 6. This robot has 55 fingers.

_____ ÷ _____ = _____

 7. This robot has 5 fingers.

_____ ÷ _____ = _____

 **8.** This robot has 15 fingers.

_____ ÷ _____ = _____

 9. This robot has 35 fingers.

_____ ÷ _____ = _____

 **10.** This robot has 40 fingers.

_____ ÷ _____ = _____

Who needs the most gloves? _____

Name _____   Date _____

Division: Facts to 12

Matchmaker Math

Use a little division to help Cupid's arrow find the right heart! Each arrow has a problem and one of the hearts has the answer. Just connect each problem to its answer and you'll have matches made in math heaven!

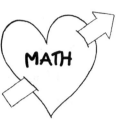

1. 36 ÷ 4 =
2. 24 ÷ 2 =
3. 64 ÷ 8 =
4. 63 ÷ 9 =
5. 33 ÷ 11 =
6. 77 ÷ 7 =
7. 10 ÷ 10 =
8. 16 ÷ 8 =
9. 60 ÷ 12 =
10. 60 ÷ 6 =
11. 36 ÷ 6 =
12. 28 ÷ 7 =

12
3
1
6
2
4
9
5
7
8
11
10

Division: Facts to 12

Name_____ Date_____

Division Banquet

Time to divide up jellybeans for the annual jellyfish jellybean banquet! The number on the cards tells you how many jellyfish will share each jar of jellybeans. Divide the number of jellybeans in the jar by the number of jellyfish. Write your equations and answers on the blanks provided.

1. ____ ÷ ____ = _____
   (56, 8 jellyfish)

2. ____ ÷ ____ = _____
   (144, 12 jellyfish)

3. ____ ÷ ____ = _____
   (72, 9 jellyfish)

4. ____ ÷ ____ = _____
   (24, 6 jellyfish)

5. ____ ÷ ____ = _____
   (60, 5 jellyfish)

6. ____ ÷ ____ = _____
   (18, 2 jellyfish)

7. ____ ÷ ____ = _____
   (49, 7 jellyfish)

8. ____ ÷ ____ = _____
   (120, 10 jellyfish)

9. ____ ÷ ____ = _____
   (121, 11 jellyfish)

10. ____ ÷ ____ = _____
    (30, 3 jellyfish)

Division: Facts to 12

Name_____ Date_____

Inspector Widget

Inspector Widget is looking for a super sleuth to add to his team of detectives at the Who Dunnit Detective Agency, and he is giving each candidate a test. Sherlock Holmes took it years ago and scored a perfect 16! Let's see how you do.

Do the division problems. Then look for the answers in word form in the story below. Circle each word. If you get the same answer to more than one division problem, it will appear in the story once for each answer. The first one has been done for you.

77 ÷ 7 = __11__   72 ÷ 9 = _____   48 ÷ 12 = _____   49 ÷ 7 = _____

50 ÷ 10 = _____   72 ÷ 12 = _____   8 ÷ 8 = _____   27 ÷ 9 = _____

40 ÷ 4 = _____   81 ÷ 9 = _____   30 ÷ 6 = _____   56 ÷ 8 = _____

12 ÷ 12 = _____   60 ÷ 6 = _____   22 ÷ 11 = _____   48 ÷ 6 = _____

Toni Terry the sixth-grade teacher at Five Forks School was mad. Her stack of homework papers was missing. She picked up the phone to call Who Dunnit Detective Agency, but there was no dial tone. In fact, it was dead.

Toni Terry began to worry. It was eight o'clock at night and storming outside, and she was by herself at school. Just then the lights went out. Ms. Terry was so frightened that she screamed seven times.

That's when I came along. Let me introduce myself, I'm Inspector Jane Gelfour, and I don't go anywhere without my canine sidekick, Clue.

That night we saw a suspicious hooded figure running toward the park's entrance tunnel even though the park was closed. He dropped seven papers as he slid out of sight. The papers were from Toni Terry's class. There was something fishy going on. We went to Five Forks School to investigate.

That's when we heard Toni Terry scream. That caught our attention. It won't surprise you that she bolted out of the school with the speed of a freight train, jumped into her car, and drove off. As she did, a note fluttered from her car window. It read:

> Ms. Terry,
> I took your papers to grade so you don't have to work late tonight. Reset your clock in the morning. Tonight is the night they're turning off the electricity and phones so they can rewire the computer lab.
> Your Student Teacher,
> Seth Reeds

How many words did you find?

Division: 1-Digit Divisor

Name _____ Date _____

Bargain Shopper

Goldie's Garden Center and Nelson's Nursery are having a sale on flowering bushes. Read the signs. Then write the price per bush. For each number, circle the better deal.

	Goldie's Garden Center		Nelson's Nursery
1.	4 for $12	or	7 for $28
2.	8 for $56	or	9 for $72
3.	4 for $64	or	3 for $45
4.	5 for $30	or	4 for $20
5.	2 for $30	or	3 for $42
6.	7 for $77	or	10 for $100

1. _____   _____
2. _____   _____
3. _____   _____
4. _____   _____
5. _____   _____
6. _____   _____

Division: 1-Digit Divisor

Name_____ Date_____

Teacher's Pet

The science teacher brought in a dog to help her in class. What kind of dog do you think it is? To find out, do the division problems. Then write the code letter beside your answer on the correct lines at the bottom of the page. The first one has been done for you.

$8\overline{)728}$ = 91 **L**

$3\overline{)606}$ **R**

$6\overline{)306}$ **Y**

$4\overline{)436}$ **E**

$9\overline{)6{,}354}$ **T**

$9\overline{)918}$ **I**

$8\overline{)488}$ **B**

$2\overline{)248}$ **O**

$3\overline{)129}$ **V**

$7\overline{)560}$ **A**

__ __ __ __ __ __ __ __ __ __
80 91 80 61 124 202 80 706 124 202 51

__ __ __ __ __ __ __ __ __
202 109 706 202 102 109 43 109 202

29

Division: 1-Digit Divisor, Remainder

Name_____ Date_____

Dial an Answer

Why does Dennis the Duck love surfing the Internet? Find out the answer by replacing the remainder in each division problem with the letter from the telephone code. Then write the letters at the bottom of the page. The first one has been done for you.

1 A	2 E	3 H
4 B	5 F	6 S
7 D	8 W	9 X
* M	0 T	# R

1. 7)38 = 5 r 3 H

2. 8)66 = __ r __ __

3. 9)21 = __ r __ __

4. 3)22 = __ r __ __

5. 8)38 = __ r __ __

6. 9)89 = __ r __ __

7. 6)20 = __ r __ __

8. 5)34 = __ r __ __

9. 7)53 = __ r __ __

10. 4)22 = __ r __ __

11. 8)79 = __ r __ __

12. 6)17 = __ r __ __

13. 3)14 = __ r __ __

14. 9)29 = __ r __ __

15. 2)16 = __ r __ __

H __ __ __ __ __
1 2 3 4 5

__ __ __ __ __ __   __ __ __ __
6 7 8 9 10 11 12 13 14 15

Division: 1-Digit Divisor, Remainder

Name_____ Date_____

Hungry Astronaut

Which meal does the astronaut like the best? To find out, follow these simple directions. Do the division problems. Find the correct answer inside the space shuttle. Circle the corresponding letter. The circled letters spell out the answer.

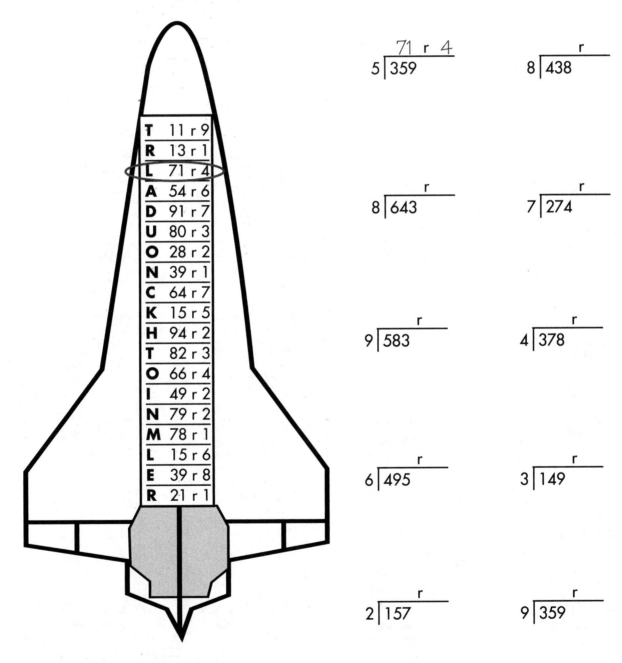

$$5\overline{)359} \quad 71\ r\ 4$$

$$8\overline{)438} \quad r$$

$$8\overline{)643} \quad r$$

$$7\overline{)274} \quad r$$

$$9\overline{)583} \quad r$$

$$4\overline{)378} \quad r$$

$$6\overline{)495} \quad r$$

$$3\overline{)149} \quad r$$

$$2\overline{)157} \quad r$$

$$9\overline{)359} \quad r$$

Inside shuttle:
T 11 r 9
R 13 r 1
L 71 r 4 (circled)
A 54 r 6
D 91 r 7
U 80 r 3
O 28 r 2
N 39 r 1
C 64 r 7
K 15 r 5
H 94 r 2
T 82 r 3
O 66 r 4
I 49 r 2
N 79 r 2
M 78 r 1
L 15 r 6
E 39 r 8
R 21 r 1

The astronaut likes

L _ _ _ _   _ _ _ _ **best!**

31

Division: 1- & 2-Digit Divisors

Name_____ Date_____

Chocolate-Chip Challenge

In this cookie contest, it's not the chef with the biggest cookie who wins. The chef who wins is the one who fits the most chocolate chips in each of his or her cookies. To find the winner, divide the number of chocolate chips by the number of cookies. (Each chef divided the chips evenly among their own cookies.)

Chef 1
65 chips,
5 cookies

____ chips in each cookie

Chef 4
900 chips,
50 cookies

____ chips in each cookie

Chef 7
56 chips,
8 cookies

____ chips in each cookie

Chef 10
150 chips,
3 cookies

____ chips in each cookie

Chef 2
180 chips,
12 cookies

____ chips in each cookie

Chef 5
144 chips,
6 cookies

____ chips in each cookie

Chef 8
84 chips,
4 cookies

____ chips in each cookie

Chef 11
702 chips,
18 cookies

____ chips in each cookie

Chef 3
840 chips,
14 cookies

____ chips in each cookie

Chef 6
56 chips,
7 cookies

____ chips in each cookie

Chef 9
132 chips,
11 cookies

____ chips in each cookie

Chef 12
1,452 chips,
66 cookies

____ chips in each cookie

Which chef won the contest? _____

How many chips were in each of this chef's cookies? _____

Division: 1-Digit Divisor, 3-Digit Quotient

Name_____ Date_____

Crisscross Number Puzzles

Solve the division problems. Each of the six 3-digit quotients fit into the puzzle below. One digit must be placed in each box to form a 3-digit number in each row (from left to right) and each column (from top to bottom). The clues will help you decide where to place the numbers.

$8\overline{)1{,}112}$ $3\overline{)2{,}394}$ $6\overline{)3{,}162}$

$4\overline{)2{,}056}$ $9\overline{)4{,}212}$ $5\overline{)1{,}180}$

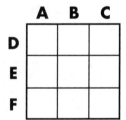

CLUES
A. The middle digit is 1.
B. The first digit is even.
C. The first digit is odd AND greater than 5.
D. The last digit is odd.
E. The last digit is 9.
F. The first digit is even.

Follow the same instructions for the puzzle below. Be careful—it only has two clues.

$5\overline{)3{,}745}$ $4\overline{)956}$ $9\overline{)1{,}638}$

$7\overline{)6{,}048}$ $3\overline{)1{,}689}$ $8\overline{)1{,}256}$

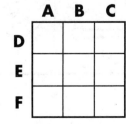

CLUES
B. The last digit is even AND less than 6.
D. The last digit is 2.

Professor Dee Vision

I bet you've never taken a final exam like the one Dee Vision, a math professor at Purdue University, has planned for her students. She's hidden each of the answers to the test somewhere in her trash heap of an office. The first student to sort through the rubbish and find all of the answers gets a Wizard Calculator. Do you want to join in on the fun? Just solve the math problems on the test below and let the search begin! Find and circle the answers in the office.

27 ⟌ 243   18 ⟌ 198   31 ⟌ 155   74 ⟌ 444

55 ⟌ 220   49 ⟌ 343   64 ⟌ 192   93 ⟌ 186

19 ⟌ 152   65 ⟌ 975   39 ⟌ 507   82 ⟌ 984

63 ⟌ 882   19 ⟌ 190   16 ⟌ 272   56 ⟌ 896

Division: 2-Digit Divisors, 2-Digit Quotients

Name_____ Date_____

Pirate's Treasure

Black-Eyed John has found a treasure map written in code. Help him break the code and find the long-lost treasure. Solve each multiplication or division problem. Write the letters spelling each product or quotient in the puzzle. The first one has been done for you.

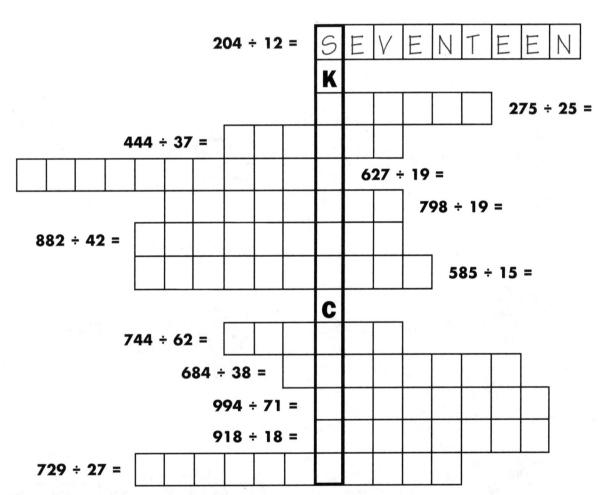

When Black-Eyed John discovered the destination written in pencil, you could hear him shout, "Yo-ho-ho and a pack of gum,

S K _ _ _ _ _ _ _   C _ _ _ _ _ _

Here we come!"

35

Division: 2-Digit Divisor, 2-Digit Quotient, Remainder

Name _____ Date _____

Across the Great Divide

These cows are being herded north to Descartes Ranch. But they got lost! How many miles does each cow have to go to get home? To find out, solve each division problem.

 **1.** 15) 4,821

 **5.** 25) 11,716

 **2.** 42) 8,412

 **6.** 50) 7,160

 3. 63) 12,666

 7. 13) 15,400

 4. 84) 8,408

 8. 19) 10,170

Which cow has to go the farthest? _____

36

Name_____ Date_____

Division: Mixed Operations

All Mixed Up

Penelope is having a bad day. She was creating a math test on her computer. All of a sudden she hit the wrong key, and the numbers got mixed up. The divisors, dividends, and quotients are scattered around the screen.

Can you put the numbers back together so that when you divide the dividend by the divisor, you get the right quotient? (If I were you, I'd use a calculator to help unscramble this mess!)

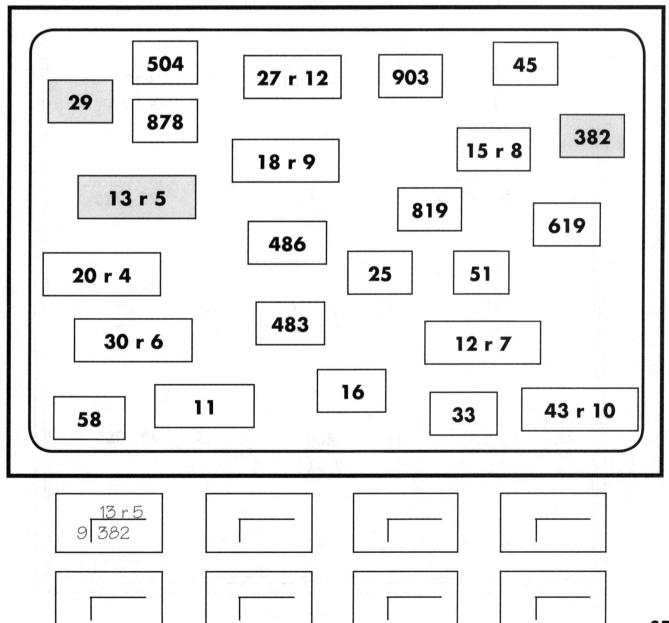

37

Mixed Practice: Multiplication & Division

Name _____ Date _____

Multiplication & Division Review

Use all of your multiplication and division skills to answer these questions as quickly—and correctly—as possible!

1. 13)676

2. 84
   × 84

3. 18)828

4. 27
   × 3

5. 16)544

6. 640
   × 46

7. 16)624

8. 17
   × 71

9. 22)726

10. 11
    × 32

11. 17)510

12. 999
    × 9

13. 9)477

14. 365
    × 52

15. 19)361

Mixed Practice: Multiplication & Division, Money

Name_____ Date_____

Five and Dime and Quarter Store

No matter what the price is, you can only pay in quarters, dimes, or nickels at this store. Answer each question below. When you've finished, use your answers to solve the riddle.

1. An inflatable soccer ball costs $10.

　　a. How many dimes does the ball cost? _____ (H)

　　b. How many quarters does the ball cost? _____ (U)

2. Cassie needs a new guitar. She has saved $100.

　　a. How many quarters can she spend on the guitar? _____ (C)

　　b. How many dimes can she spend on the guitar? _____ (A)

　　c. How many nickels can she spend on the guitar? _____ (D)

3. The "Change-opoly" board game costs $11.75.

　　a. How many quarters is that? _____ (G)

　　b. How many nickels? _____ (S)

4. Alice spent 87 nickels on a book.

　　a. How much is that in dollars and cents? _____ (B)

5. Dean wants to buy a pair of tennis shoes that are on sale for $32. He has 130 quarters to spend.

　　a. How much money can he spend? _____ (K)

　　b. How many quarters will he have left over after he buys the shoes? _____ (O)

　　c. How many nickels is that? _____ (L)

　　d. How many dimes is that? _____ (T)

Q: Why did the chef go to the bank?

A: He needed some " ____ ____ ____ ____ ____ " !
　　　　　　　　　　　2,000　2　40　47　100

39

Mixed Practice: Multiplication & Division, Word Problems

Name_____ Date_____

Read All About It...Carefully!

Math makes the headlines! Use your multiplication and division skills to find out more. Remember to read the questions carefully before responding.

THE MATH DAILY

Card Collecting Craze Hits!
1. Mark has collected 127 baseball cards.
   a. Alec has collected 3 times as many baseball cards as Mark. How many cards has Alec collected? _____
   b. Erica has collected 5 times as many baseball cards as Alec. How many cards has Erica collected? _____
   c. Susan has collected 4 times as many baseball cards as Mark. How many cards has Susan collected? _____

Homework Division
2. Veronica has 276 math problems to do! Luckily she has plenty of time. She decides to divide them up.
   a. If Veronica divides her problems over 4 days, how many math problems must she do each day?
   _____
   b. If Veronica divides her problems over 3 days, how many math problems must she do each day?
   _____
   c. If Veronica divides her math problems over 6 days, how many must she do each day? _____

Big Games This Weekend!
3. The school's athletes need to divide into teams for the big games this weekend. There are three sports and each sport needs a different number of players on each team. There are 540 athletes.
   a. How many teams of 9 players can be made? _____
   b. How many teams of 6 players can be made? _____
   c. How many teams of 10 players can be made? _____

Seashell Goldmine Uncovered!
4. During his summer vacation, Scott spends a week at the beach with his family collecting seashells. On Sunday, he finds 13 seashells.
   a. On Monday, he has 5 times as many as he had on Sunday. How many seashells does he have now? _____
   b. On Tuesday, he has 3 times as many as he had on Monday. How many seashells does he have now? _____
   c. On Wednesday, he finds 11 times as many as he did on Sunday. How many seashells did he find? _____

Estimation: Multiplication

Name_____ Date_____

Tic-tac-toe

This tic-tac-toe game gives you all the answers you need to win. All you have to do is find the row, column, or diagonal that is the winner.

Here's how: Look at the problems on the game board. To find the answers, round each 3-digit number to the nearest ten and each 4-digit number to the nearest hundred, and then multiply. You don't need to round 1-digit numbers. See if your answer matches one in the answer box. If it does, write the answer on the line under the problem. When you find a row, column, or diagonal of answers, draw a circle around the problems.

504 × 5	385 × 3	714 × 8
689 × 2	209 × 6	1,742 × 2
1,119 × 7	2,894 × 4	3,046 × 5

ANSWER BOX

5,680

116,000

3,500

1,260

2,400

1,390

7,710

1,180

7,700

Congratulations! You've won the game.

41

Estimation: Division

Name_____ Date_____

Math Hunt

Petunia is always losing things. Yesterday, it was her glasses. (She found them on top of her head.) Today she's missing the answers to her estimation test. The answers are in this pile of letters. Please help her find them.

Here's how: Estimate the quotients to the division problems. Round 3-digit numbers to the nearest ten and 4-digit numbers to the nearest hundred. Then see if you can find all 12 estimated answers written in the pile of letters. (They're written forward, backward, and diagonally.) Circle the answers.

$5\overline{)447}$ $6\overline{)241}$ $9\overline{)542}$ $3\overline{)146}$

$8\overline{)639}$ $7\overline{)144}$ $5\overline{)351}$ $8\overline{)5,561}$

$5\overline{)4,520}$ $4\overline{)1,589}$ $2\overline{)1,595}$ $3\overline{)1,847}$

```
F  T  L  G  Q  S  X  C  V  T  I  N  S  S
O  O  D  E  R  D  N  U  H  T  H  G  I  E
U  M  R  H  M  O  O  I  P  R  X  U  X  V
R  Y  Z  T  V  B  G  U  N  Y  D  D  T  E
H  O  N  L  Y  B  V  C  S  E  T  P  Y  N
U  R  Y  T  H  G  I  E  S  S  T  F  H  T
N  I  N  E  H  U  N  D  R  E  D  Y  I  Y
D  E  R  D  N  U  H  N  E  V  E  S  G  F
R  A  K  J  N  C  G  V  T  B  Q  W  E  T
E  A  E  O  T  W  E  N  T  Y  T  U  O  P
D  E  R  D  N  U  H  X  I  S  K  H  J  K
```

42

Estimation: Multiplication & Division

Name_____ Date_____

 # Bees, Please!

Buzz estimates that his large hives each have 150 bees and his small hives each have 75 bees. Answer these questions by using your estimation skills. Circle the estimate that makes sense.

1. Down by the swamp, Buzz finds 5 small hives and 2 large hives.
   a. How many bees are in the small hives?   400   or   4,000
   b. How many bees are in the large hives?   30   or   300
   c. How many bees in all are down by the swamp?   700   or   200

2. Behind the house, Buzz finds 3 small hives and 4 large hives.
   a. How many bees are in the small hives?   25   or   200
   b. How many bees are in the large hives?   600   or   6,000
   c. How many bees in all are behind the house?   800   or   80

3. Next to the briar patch, Buzz finds 6 small hives and 6 large hives.
   a. How many bees are in the small hives?   40   or   400
   b. How many bees are in the large hives?   9,000   or   900
   c. How many bees in all are next to the briar patch?   1,300   or   1,600

4. In his old pickup truck, Buzz finds 8 small hives and 3 large hives.
   a. How many bees are in the small hives?   60   or   600
   b. How many bees are in the large hives?   45   or   450
   c. How many bees in all are in his old pickup truck?   1,000   or   2,000

5. Which location has the most bees? _____

Fractions: Naming Simple Fractions

Name_____ Date_____

Fractions With Cheese

Fractions for lunch! Well, even if you don't have an appetite for pickle pizza, we hope you'll have an appetite for math! Answer the questions below.

1. What fraction of the pizza has pretzels? _____

2. What fraction of the pizza has gumdrops? _____

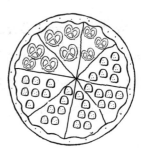

3. What fraction of the pizza has marshmallows? _____

4. What fraction of the pizza has peanuts? _____

5. What fraction of the pizza has popcorn? _____

6. What fraction of the pizza has pickles? _____

7. What fraction of the pizza has potato chips? _____

8. What fraction of the pizza has bean sprouts? _____

9. What fraction of the pizza has strawberries? _____

10. What fraction of the pizza has grapes? _____

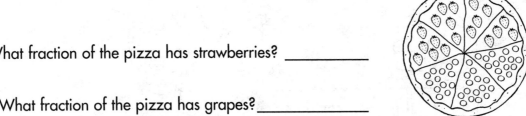

Fractions: Simplifying Fractions

Name_____ Date_____

Fractions Are a Breeze

Sail into fractions by renaming each fraction below in lowest terms.
If the fraction is equal to 1/2 or 3/4, shade the box blue.
If the fraction is equal to 1/4, shade the box yellow.
If the fraction is equal to 1/3, shade the box green.
If the boxes are colored correctly, a picture will appear.

$\frac{3}{6}$	$\frac{2}{8}$	$\frac{21}{42}$	$\frac{75}{150}$	$\frac{31}{62}$	$\frac{11}{22}$	$\frac{7}{14}$
$\frac{50}{100}$	$\frac{9}{36}$	$\frac{11}{44}$	$\frac{32}{64}$	$\frac{30}{60}$	$\frac{6}{12}$	$\frac{60}{120}$
$\frac{4}{8}$	$\frac{7}{28}$	$\frac{16}{64}$	$\frac{3}{12}$	$\frac{8}{16}$	$\frac{40}{80}$	$\frac{12}{16}$
$\frac{9}{18}$	$\frac{25}{100}$	$\frac{6}{24}$	$\frac{8}{32}$	$\frac{19}{76}$	$\frac{48}{64}$	$\frac{5}{10}$
$\frac{10}{20}$	$\frac{17}{68}$	$\frac{12}{48}$	$\frac{13}{52}$	$\frac{20}{80}$	$\frac{25}{100}$	$\frac{14}{28}$
$\frac{35}{70}$	$\frac{8}{32}$	$\frac{10}{40}$	$\frac{15}{60}$	$\frac{40}{160}$	$\frac{14}{56}$	$\frac{5}{20}$
$\frac{21}{28}$	$\frac{12}{24}$	$\frac{40}{80}$	$\frac{15}{30}$	$\frac{33}{66}$	$\frac{15}{20}$	$\frac{75}{100}$
$\frac{5}{10}$ / $\frac{2}{6}$	$\frac{12}{36}$	$\frac{9}{27}$	$\frac{30}{90}$	$\frac{20}{60}$	$\frac{11}{33}$	$\frac{6}{18}$ / $\frac{2}{4}$
$\frac{18}{24}$	$\frac{9}{12}$ / $\frac{5}{15}$	$\frac{15}{45}$	$\frac{8}{24}$	$\frac{10}{30}$	$\frac{3}{9}$ / $\frac{6}{8}$	$\frac{30}{40}$

45

Fractions: Simplifying Fractions

Name_____ Date_____

Wake Up!

Did you know the sun has an alarm clock? To find out what it looks like, complete the picture. Find two fractions that are equivalent, and then connect them with a line. Continue connecting equivalent fractions until the picture is complete.

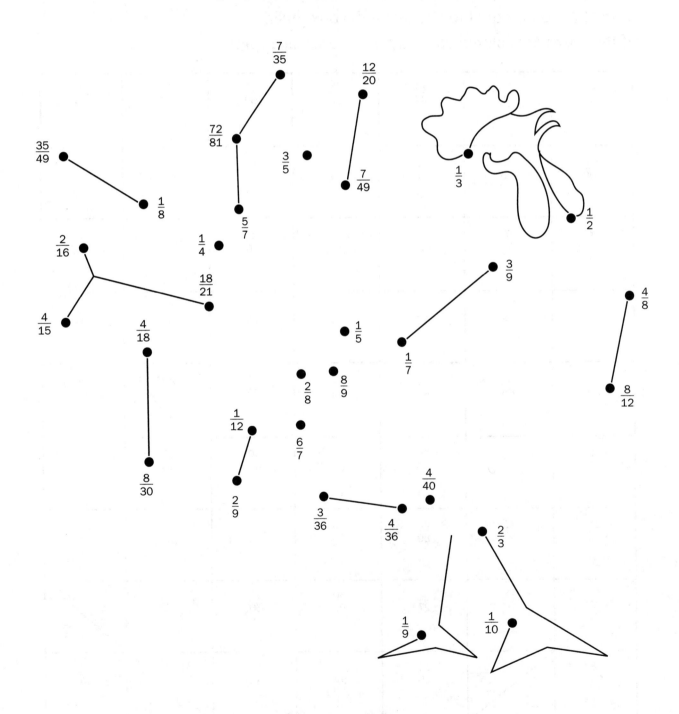

Fractions: Comparing & Ranking

Name_____ Date_____

Skyscraping Fractions

It's a bird... It's a plane... It's Fraction Man! Able to leap over tall fractions in a single bound. But which is biggest? Luckily, the buildings in Mathopolis are all labeled with fractions. First, compare the fractions, two at a time, by finding common denominators. You may have to do some fractions more than once. Write your fractions on the blank. Finally, list the fractions in order, from the smallest to the largest, in the blanks at the bottom of the paper.

Rank the fractions from smallest to largest.

___ ___ ___ ___ ___ ___ ___ ___

Fractions: Comparing & Ranking

Name _____ Date _____

Three Cheers for Fractions!

Go team! But wait—where are the cheerleaders? They're a bit confused by their fractions. You can help them line up for the big cheer. Write each cheerleader's number next to the correct mark on the sideline numberline. Then draw a line from the cheerleader to his or her number.

Fractions: Identifying Equivalent Fractions

Name _____ Date _____

Egg Hunt

Look! There are 20 eggs hidden in trees, under swings, and beside slides in the park. Each egg is filled with a surprise. Grab your basket and start the search.

Oh—one thing! Five of the eggs contain surprises all right—the kind that make you want to hold your nose.

How can you tell the eggs apart? The eggs that have fractions equivalent to 2/5 contain surprises that will make you smile. The other eggs will make you want to cry.

See if you can find and circle the 15 sweet-smelling eggs.

I hope you didn't pick up a phew (few) of those smelly eggs!

49

Fractions: Addition With Like Denominators

Name_____ Date_____

The Puzzle Factory Mystery

Mr. Clue finished detective school yesterday. Now he's working on his first assignment. Someone has stolen 100 puzzles from Plitterbum's Puzzle Factory. Wait a minute! Do you see what I see? There's a puzzle lying on the floor in pieces. Cut out the scattered pieces of the puzzle below. Place them on top of the matching pieces on the puzzle board.

Be careful—some of the shapes may fit the puzzle board but do not correctly solve the addition problem. (Don't forget to rename your answers in lowest terms.)

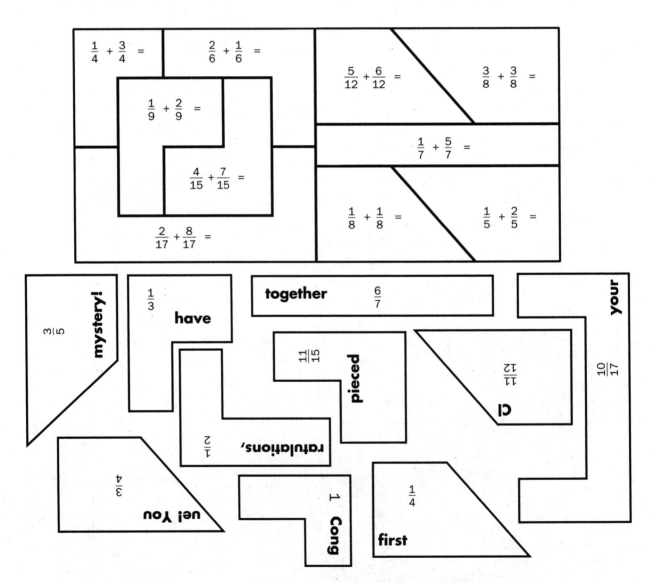

What is the mystery message on the completed puzzle?

50 _____

Fractions: Addition With Unlike Denominators

Name_____ Date_____

Going Buggy

Bugs Galore makes hundreds of stuffed bugs every year. Today the company is having problems because the bug halves are all mixed up. Can you find the right-hand side that matches the left-hand side of each bug? Circle it.

Check your answers by adding the fractions under each bug half. If the two halves match, the two fractions added together should equal 1.

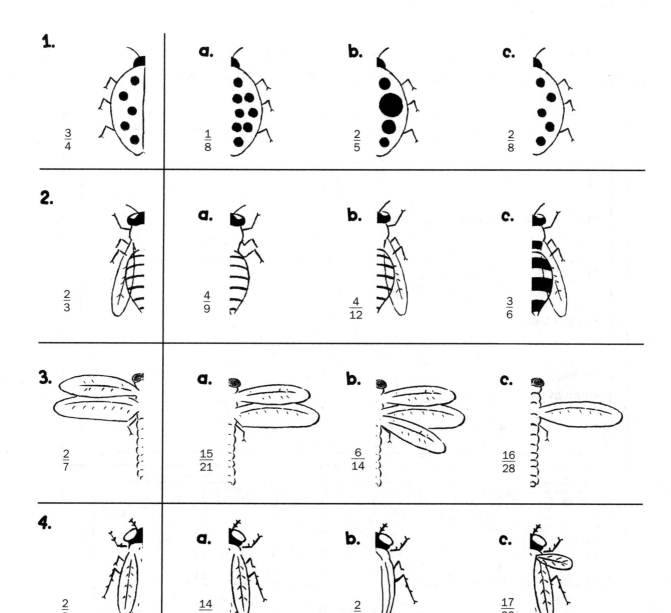

Fractions: Addition With Unlike Denominators

Name _____ Date _____

Someone's in the Attic

Tom stared at the television set, trying not to hear the wind howl and the rain beat against the roof. It was a spooky night—and he was home alone. EEEEEEEE!!!! It sounded like someone was in the attic screaming! Tom shook his head; he must be imagining things.

Tom wondered why his dad was so late getting home from work. He walked into his dad's office to look for a note. He noticed there was some kind of message on the computer screen. Does the message make sense to you?

Solve the problems. Rename all answers in lowest terms. Find the matching answer on the keyboard below, and write it above the problem. Then read the message.

| __H__ $\frac{1}{2}+\frac{1}{3}=$ | __I__ $\frac{1}{4}+\frac{2}{8}=$ | __T__ $\frac{5}{9}+\frac{1}{3}=$ | __O__ $\frac{5}{12}+\frac{1}{6}=$ | __M__ $\frac{1}{7}+\frac{1}{21}=$ |

I'm home from work early. I am ...

| __F__ $\frac{1}{12}+\frac{1}{3}=$ | __I__ $\frac{1}{10}+\frac{2}{5}=$ | __X__ $\frac{1}{3}+\frac{1}{9}=$ | __I__ $\frac{1}{3}+\frac{1}{6}=$ | __N__ $\frac{3}{4}+\frac{1}{8}=$ | __G__ $\frac{2}{22}+\frac{3}{11}=$ |

the broken

| __L__ $\frac{2}{15}+\frac{2}{3}=$ | __O__ $\frac{2}{12}+\frac{5}{12}=$ | __C__ $\frac{7}{20}+\frac{2}{5}=$ | __K__ $\frac{1}{4}+\frac{3}{8}=$ |

on the door in the ____ ____ ____ ____ ____ **!**

| __A__ $\frac{1}{14}+\frac{5}{7}=$ | __T__ $\frac{7}{9}+\frac{2}{18}=$ | __T__ $\frac{2}{3}+\frac{2}{9}=$ | __I__ $\frac{2}{12}+\frac{2}{6}=$ | __C__ $\frac{1}{2}+\frac{1}{4}=$ |

Keyboard:

Q $\frac{1}{7}$	W $\frac{1}{9}$	E $\frac{1}{3}$	R $\frac{1}{6}$	T $\frac{8}{9}$	Y $\frac{1}{8}$	U $\frac{3}{11}$	I $\frac{1}{2}$	O $\frac{7}{12}$	P $\frac{3}{7}$
A $\frac{11}{14}$	S $\frac{1}{11}$	D $\frac{2}{9}$	F $\frac{5}{12}$	G $\frac{4}{11}$	H $\frac{5}{6}$	J $\frac{1}{12}$	K $\frac{5}{8}$	L $\frac{4}{5}$	: ;
Z $\frac{4}{7}$	X $\frac{4}{9}$	C $\frac{3}{4}$	V $\frac{2}{7}$	B $\frac{2}{3}$	N $\frac{7}{8}$	M $\frac{4}{21}$	< ,	> .	? /

52

Fractions: Subtraction With Like Denominators

Name_____ Date_____

Curious Critter

What would you get if you crossed a tadpole and a cow? To find out, solve the subtraction problems below. Rename them in lowest terms. Find the dot with the first answer and connect it to the dot with the next answer. Continue connecting the dots until the picture is complete. Find your answers under the lines at the bottom of the page. Write their letters on the lines.

$\frac{6}{14} - \frac{1}{14}$ $\frac{4}{9} - \frac{3}{9}$ $\frac{11}{12} - \frac{9}{12}$ $\frac{7}{10} - \frac{2}{10}$ $\frac{25}{28} - \frac{5}{28}$ $\frac{11}{15} - \frac{1}{15}$ $\frac{9}{20} - \frac{2}{20}$ $\frac{19}{24} - \frac{8}{24}$

$\frac{7}{13} - \frac{2}{13}$ $\frac{8}{9} - \frac{4}{9}$ $\frac{12}{17} - \frac{6}{17}$ $\frac{13}{14} - \frac{11}{14}$ $\frac{6}{16} - \frac{1}{16}$ $\frac{7}{19} - \frac{2}{19}$ $\frac{7}{8} - \frac{4}{8}$

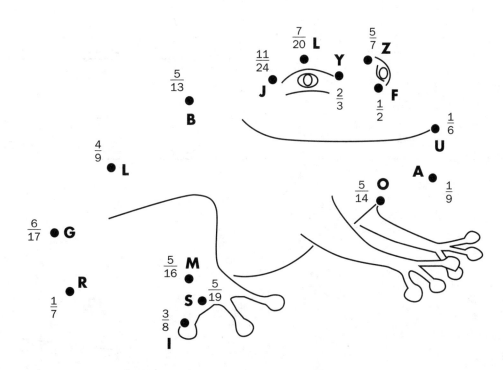

Write your answer to the riddle below.

___ ___ ___ ___ ___ ___ ___ ___
$\frac{5}{13}$ $\frac{1}{6}$ $\frac{7}{20}$ $\frac{4}{9}$ $\frac{1}{2}$ $\frac{1}{7}$ $\frac{5}{14}$ $\frac{6}{17}$

53

Fractions: Subtraction With Unlike Denominators

Name _____ Date _____

Underwater Mystery

Detective Lawson handed the crumpled paper to the math professor. "We know the Crown Jewels are hidden somewhere in one of the aquarium tanks," she said, "but we don't know which one. You're our last hope, professor. If you can break the code on this note, we'll know exactly where to look."

After the detective left, the professor took off his glasses and rubbed his eyes as he thought about the puzzle. Crash! His glasses slid off the desk and smashed into pieces on the concrete floor.

Jeepers, creepers! Now the professor can't see. It looks like you're the only one left to break the code. Find the answers to the subtraction problems. Then connect the dots. Follow the same order as the answers, and you'll break the code!

$$\frac{6}{7} - \frac{1}{4} \qquad \frac{4}{5} - \frac{1}{2} \qquad \frac{8}{9} - \frac{2}{3} \qquad \frac{11}{12} - \frac{1}{2} \qquad \frac{3}{4} - \frac{1}{2} \qquad \frac{5}{6} - \frac{2}{3} \qquad \frac{6}{10} - \frac{1}{4} \qquad \frac{15}{16} - \frac{1}{3}$$

$$\frac{2}{3} - \frac{1}{2} \qquad \frac{7}{8} - \frac{3}{4} \qquad \frac{6}{11} - \frac{1}{2} \qquad \frac{4}{5} - \frac{1}{4} \qquad \frac{5}{8} - \frac{1}{3} \qquad \frac{7}{9} - \frac{3}{5} \qquad \frac{4}{7} - \frac{1}{2}$$

· 29/48   · 5/12   · 2/9   · 3/10   · 17/28

· 7/20   · 1/6   · 1/4

· 1/6

· 1/22   · 11/20   · 1/14

· 1/8   · 8/45

· 7/24

54

Fraction Factory

Welcome to the Fraction Factory! Our worker is putting these fractions together trying to get to the number "1." How many fractions does it take for the worker to get to 1? Here's how to find out. First, add and subtract the fractions in order from left to right along the conveyor belt. When the fractions add up to "1," you can stop. Next, help put together some more fractions to equal 1. Give your answer in simplest terms.

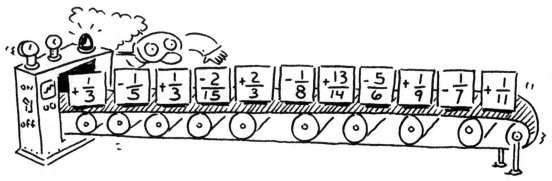

How many fractions added up to number 1? _____

1. $\dfrac{4}{5} + \underline{} - \dfrac{3}{10} = 1$

2. $\dfrac{3}{3} + \underline{} - \dfrac{5}{6} = 1$

3. $\dfrac{11}{22} + \underline{} - \dfrac{1}{44} = 1$

4. $\dfrac{5}{25} + \dfrac{1}{4} - \dfrac{2}{40} + \underline{} = 1$

5. $\dfrac{3}{4} + \underline{} - \dfrac{1}{12} + \dfrac{30}{60} - \dfrac{15}{30} = 1$

Fractions: Identifying Equivalent Improper Fractions & Mixed Numbers

Name_____ Date_____

The World's Biggest Ant

What is the biggest ant in the world? To find out, draw a straight line between each improper fraction and the equivalent mixed fraction. Can you complete the drawing by connecting the rest of the dots? Find your answers under the lines at the bottom of the page. Write their letters on the lines.

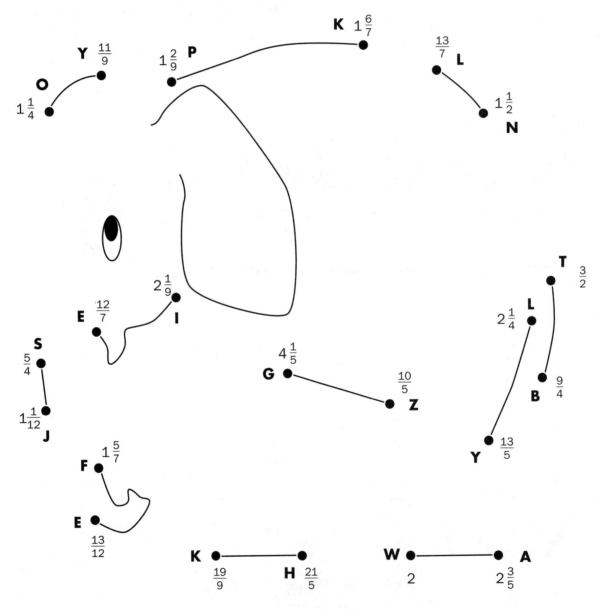

Write your answer to the riddle below.

__ __ __ __ __ __ __ __
$\frac{12}{7}$ $\frac{13}{7}$ $\frac{13}{12}$ $1\frac{2}{9}$ $\frac{21}{5}$ $2\frac{3}{5}$ $1\frac{1}{2}$ $\frac{3}{2}$

Fractions: Identifying Equivalent Improper Fractions & Mixed Numbers

Name_____ Date_____

Fishy Business

What kind of cat never meows? To find out the answer to the riddle, match the improper fractions in the box below with the mixed numbers in the picture puzzle. Then shade the mixed numbers.

$\dfrac{89}{8}$ $\dfrac{10}{3}$ $\dfrac{3}{2}$ $\dfrac{79}{12}$ $\dfrac{19}{5}$ $\dfrac{68}{9}$

$\dfrac{9}{8}$ $\dfrac{36}{5}$ $\dfrac{7}{2}$ $\dfrac{16}{11}$ $\dfrac{37}{4}$ $\dfrac{7}{4}$

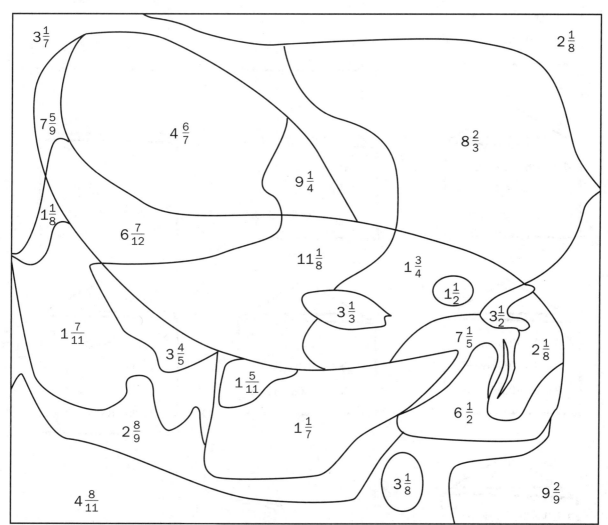

Write your answer to the riddle on the line below.

_____

57

Decimals: Place Value

Name_____ Date_____

Decimal Construction

These construction workers have a big job ahead of them. They're building decimals. You can help. Read the clues on each house. Then write the correct decimal on the roof of each house.

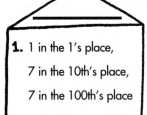

1. 1 in the 1's place,
7 in the 10th's place,
7 in the 100th's place

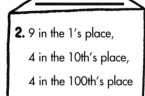

2. 9 in the 1's place,
4 in the 10th's place,
4 in the 100th's place

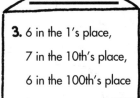

3. 6 in the 1's place,
7 in the 10th's place,
6 in the 100th's place

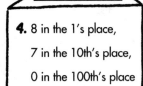

4. 8 in the 1's place,
7 in the 10th's place,
0 in the 100th's place

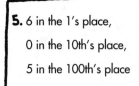

5. 6 in the 1's place,
0 in the 10th's place,
5 in the 100th's place

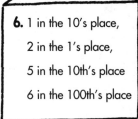

6. 1 in the 10's place,
2 in the 1's place,
5 in the 10th's place
6 in the 100th's place

7. 3 in the 1's place,
0 in the 10th's place,
9 in the 100th's place

8. 0 in the 1's place,
1 in the 10th's place,
5 in the 100th's place

9. 2 in the 10's place,
4 in the 1's place,
9 in the 10th's place
9 in the 100th's place

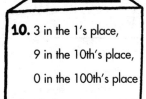

10. 3 in the 1's place,
9 in the 10th's place,
0 in the 100th's place

58

Decimals: Place Value

Name_____   Date_____

Million Dollar Winner

Congratulations! You may be our grand-prize winner of $1 million! If you're the first person to call this special number, you can pick up your winnings today!

Hold the phone. This isn't a telephone number. Or is it? Use the clues below to find out the phone number.

1. 14.79 — The number in the tenths place is the last number in the million-dollar phone number.

2. 4.986 — None of the numbers in this decimal are in the million-dollar phone number.

3. 1.9 — If you add $\frac{1}{10}$ to this number, you will get the first number in the mystery number.

4. 3.95 — The number in the hundredths place is the second and third number in the million-dollar number.

5. 4.981 — One of these numbers is the fourth number in the mystery number.

6. 9.003 — The number in the thousandth place is used twice in the mystery number.

Write the telephone number on the lines below.

____ ____ ____ — ____ ____ ____ ____

Mystery at the Abandoned Library

Just before midnight, Tom and Elizabeth pushed open the creaky door to the decaying library. Their flashlights lit up row after row of dusty books.

"There they are," whispered Elizabeth as she pointed to the towering bookshelf in the mystery section.

"You're right—the key to the jewelry case is inside one of the mystery books," said Tom. "I just wish we knew which one."

"These books are all messed up," said Elizabeth. "Maybe if we put them back in order, we'll get a clue."

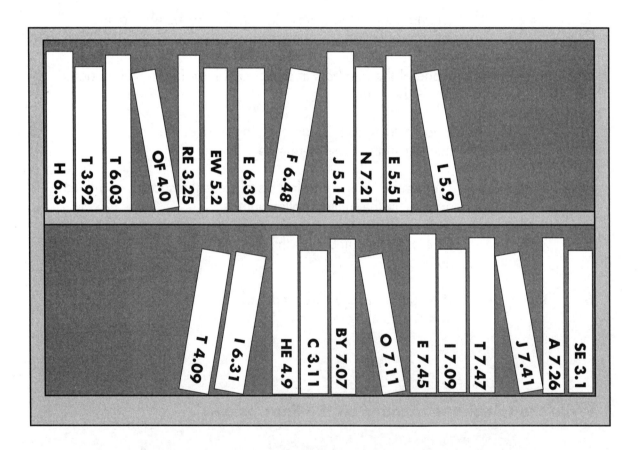

On a separate piece of paper, order the books from least to greatest, according to the decimal numbers. The letters on the book spines will spell out the clue. Write the clue on the line below.

Decimals: Comparing & Ranking

Name_____ Date_____

Line Up

It's time to audition for the school play, but our stage manager has lost the audition schedule! Luckily, our performers still have their numbers. Decimals, of course. Rank the decimals from lowest to highest. Then write each decimal in its space on the audition schedule. The first one is done for you.

Audition Schedule

12:45	**.0900**
1 o'clock	_____
1:15	_____
1:30	_____
1:45	_____
2 o'clock	_____
2:15	_____
2:30	_____
2:45	_____
3 o'clock	_____

Decimals: Rounding

Name_____ Date_____

Runaway Dogs

Freda's twin dogs have run away. She's at the dog pound hunting for Trixie and Dixie, who look exactly alike. Can you find the dogs? Check your answer by rounding each decimal to the nearest whole number. If the decimals round to the same number, the dogs above them are Freda's.

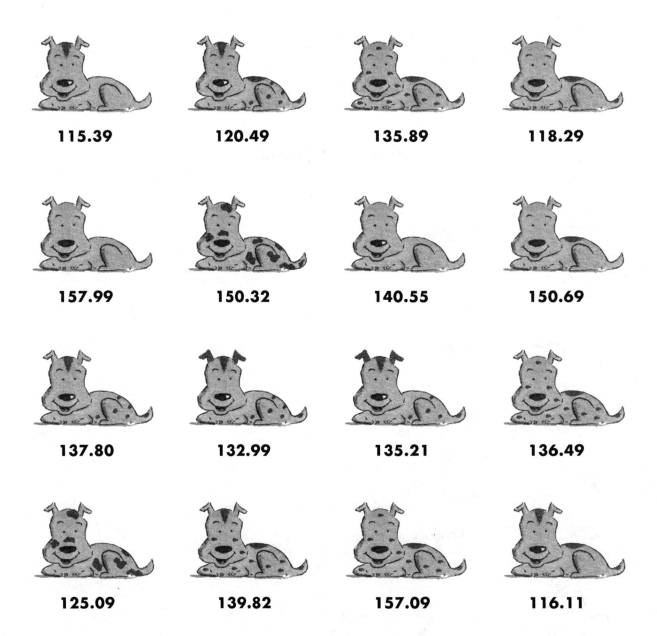

115.39	120.49	135.89	118.29
157.99	150.32	140.55	150.69
137.80	132.99	135.21	136.49
125.09	139.82	157.09	116.11

Decimals: Addition

Name_____ Date_____

Greedy Gretchen

Which path can Greedy Gretchen take from her house to the bank to collect the most gold? First, fill in the Gold Totals chart below. Then, draw a line to show the path with the most gold.

Gold Totals

Path 1	Path 2	Path 3	Path 4

63

Decimals: Addition

Name_____ Date_____

Funny Bunnies

Tilson's Toy Company ordered nine identical stuffed animals from Bunnies 'R' Us. When the bunnies arrived, only two of them were alike. Can you find the two identical bunnies and circle them?

Check your answers by solving the addition problem under each bunny. The identical bunnies have the same answer.

ID Number:
74.3 + 18.4 = _____

ID Number:
14.8 + 11.2 = _____

ID Number:
107.9 + 114.3 = _____

ID Number:
104.1 + 95.5 = _____

ID Number:
49 + 12.6 = _____

ID Number:
132.2 + 94.9 = _____

ID Number:
93.1 + 15.9 = _____

ID Number:
199.9 + 98.7 = _____

ID Number:
154.1 + 68.1 = _____

Name_____ Date_____

Shark Subtraction

Solve each subtraction problem. Then write the answer in the crossword puzzle. Each decimal point occupies a square.

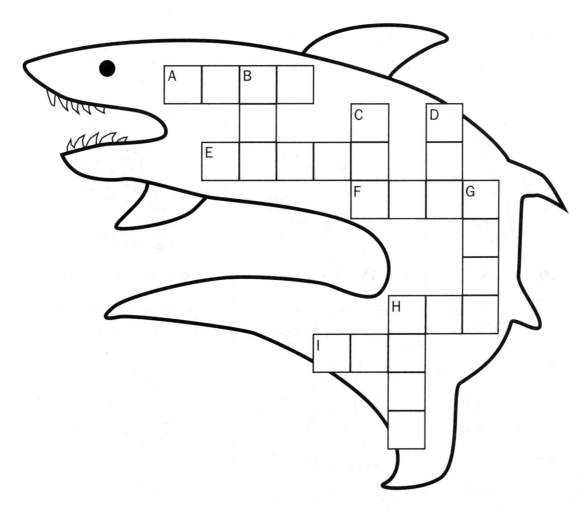

Across

A. 6.52 − 4.55 = _____

E. 43.91 − 5.19 = _____

F. 9.41 − 5.45 = _____

H. 28 − 23.2 = _____

I. 20.4 − 12.5 = _____

Down

B. 17.5 − 7.7 = _____

C. 132.78 − 9.78 = _____

D. 10.7 − 4.8 = _____

G. 14.91 − 8.13 = _____

H. 104.3 − 54.7 = _____

Decimals: Subtraction

Name_____ Date_____

Obstinate Oscar

When Obstinate Oscar's teachers tried to teach him to read, he announced, "I don't need to know how to read. I just want to go outside and play!"

These pictures tell a story about Oscar. Can you number them in correct order? One is completed for you. Check your order by doing the subtraction problems. Order the answers from least to greatest. The order of the answers matches the correct order of the story panels.

500.7 − 259.4 =	181.9 − 67.9 =	684.6 − 425.7 =
9 611.5 − 299.7 = 311.8	311.3 − 125.7 =	137.3 − 99.3 =
209.8 − 140.3 =	895.9 − 615.8 =	472.3 − 205.1 =

I saw Oscar leaving the library with a stack of books. It looks like the best teacher for Oscar was experience!

Decimals: Subtraction, Money

Name_____ Date_____

Shopping Spree

Our shoppers are ready to go. Each of them has $99 to spend and each wants to spend as much money as possible. First, start with $99 and keep subtracting from each of your answers as long as you can. When you don't have enough money left, write the amount left over on the blank to the right. Do the same for all three shoppers.
On your mark . . . Get set . . . Subtract!

1. Heather goes to the $18.99 store.
$99 − $18.99 = _____
_____ − $18.99 = _____
_____ − $18.99 = _____
_____ − $18.99 = _____
_____ − $18.99 = _____

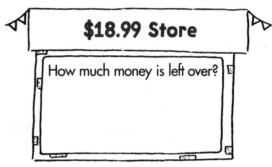

$18.99 Store
How much money is left over?

2. Lisa goes to the $19.99 store.
$99 − $19.99 = _____
_____ − $19.99 = _____
_____ − $19.99 = _____
_____ − $19.99 = _____
_____ − $19.99 = _____

$19.99 Store
How much money is left over?

3. Jack goes to the $20.99 store.
$99 − $20.99 = _____
_____ − $20.99 = _____
_____ − $20.99 = _____
_____ − $20.99 = _____
_____ − $20.99 = _____

$20.99 Store
How much money is left over?

Who has the most money left over? _____

Who spent the most money? _____

Decimals: Addition & Subtraction, Money

Name_____ Date_____

Discount Decimals

Our shoppers are coupon crazy! It's time to check out and they have their coupons ready. They each have $50. How much money will each one have left after his or her little spree? Add up how much each spends and don't forget to subtract for the coupons. Then write the amount each has left over in the blanks provided.

Shopper Number 1:

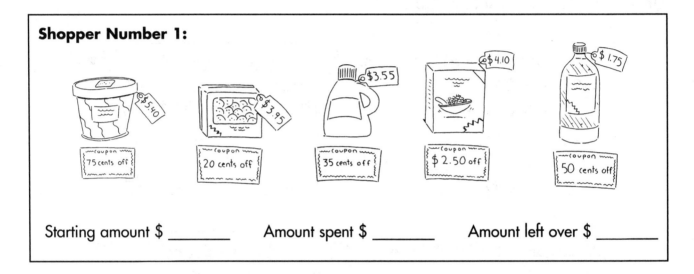

Starting amount $ _____   Amount spent $ _____   Amount left over $ _____

Shopper Number 2:

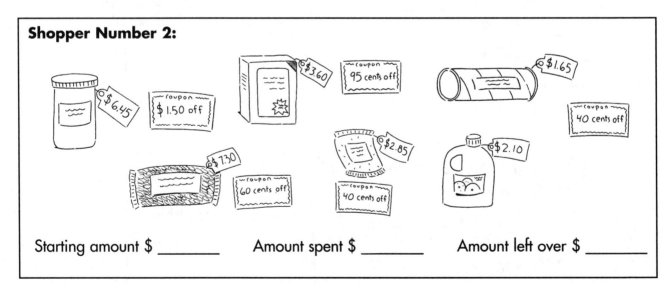

Starting amount $ _____   Amount spent $ _____   Amount left over $ _____

There are different ways to do this activity. Which way did you do it?

_____

_____

68

Batter Up

The Boomtown Batters need new baseball equipment. To find out how much the team spent for each item, multiply the amount of each item by the number of items it bought. Write each product in the crossword puzzle. Each decimal point occupies a square.

Across

A. $12.19 x 3 = _____

C. $4.95 x 9 = _____

D. $0.89 x 8 = _____

F. $1.10 x 6 = _____

G. $23.13 x 7 = _____

I. $0.94 x 8 = _____

K. $13.12 x 6 = _____

Down

A. $7.01 x 5 = _____

B. $9.45 x 6 = _____

C. $6.23 x 7 = _____

E. $0.33 x 7 = _____

H. $1.12 x 6 = _____

J. $1.25 x 2 = _____

Decimals: Multiplying Decimals by Whole Numbers, Money

Name_____ Date_____

Yikes! Moor Misstakes!

Jo Wright, an editor of the *Math Gazette*, is in a real fix. The newspaper must go to press tomorrow morning at 8 a.m. sharp, but the advertisement below has four math mistakes in it. Can you help Jo and circle each mistake?

Handley's Gloves and Shoes Is Having a SUPER SALE!

3 pairs of black leather gloves for $6.99 a pair!

(Wow—that's only $21 in all!)

Mittens, mittens, mittens! Buy 4 pairs for $6.25 a pair and get 1 pair free!

(Folks—that's only $25 for 5 pairs!)

Work Gloves! Buy them by the half dozen and save! They cost $12.75 a pair if you buy them individually. But they're $10.27 a pair when you buy them by the half dozen!

(That means a half dozen only costs $61.13!)

Sandals! Ladies casual sandals are on sale for **$7.89 a pair if you buy 4 pairs.**

(Ladies—that's only $31.50 for 4 pairs.)

Gardening Gloves! $1.99 a pair if you buy 7 pairs!

(What a buy—that's only $13.93 in all!)

Plastic Gloves: 2 pairs for a dollar!

(That's only $10.50 for 20 pairs!)

Mix and Match Shoe Sale! Buy any two pairs of shoes and get another pair—totally **FREE**. If you buy two pairs of shoes for $9.89 a pair, you can get all three pairs for only $19.78! What a deal!

Clothes Crisis

Mandy, Sandy, Candy, and Brandy are models. They each have two pieces of clothing or accessories on the clothes rack below. They have a big problem: they don't know which outfit to wear. Fortunately, the problem's been solved. Each model has a card with a number on it and these instructions: The numbers on two pieces of clothing or accessories, when multiplied together, equal the number on your card. Those are your clothes.

Get out paper, pencil, and a calculator to help you figure out who gets which outfit. Write each model's name in the box under the clothing.

Mandy	Sandy	Candy	Brandy
16.64	56.16	64.99	53.34

Top row tags: 38.1 | 21.6 | 1.3 | 9.7

Bottom row tags: 2.6 | 6.7 | 1.4 | 12.8

Answers:
- Mandy (16.64): 1.3 × 12.8
- Sandy (56.16): 21.6 × 2.6
- Candy (64.99): 9.7 × 6.7
- Brandy (53.34): 38.1 × 1.4

Decimals: Multiplying & Dividing Decimals Using a Calculator

Name_____ Date_____

Calculator Math

Get out your calculators and get ready for some multiplication and division! This time you'll be working with decimals. Once you've answered all the questions, use your answers to solve the riddle below.

1. 1.21 × 4.2 = _____ (N)

2. 4.22 ÷ 2.11 = _____ (I)

3. 12.12 × .33 = _____ (S)

4. 5.5 ÷ .25 = _____ (G)

5. 7.6 × 2.1 = _____ (P)

6. 10.10 ÷ .01 = _____ (T)

7. 5.25 × 100 = _____ (O)

8. 8.75 ÷ .5 = _____ (H)

9. 6.04 × 3 = _____ (A)

Q: What did one decimal say to the other?

A: "Get to the _____ _____ _____ _____ _____ **"!**
  15.96   525   2   5.082   1,010

72

Decimals: Converting Decimals to Fractions

Name_____ Date_____

Measure Mania

You may have heard of inches and yards, but you probably haven't heard of some of these wacky units! To find out more, convert each of the decimals to fractions. Then find that fraction in the list on the right. The correct unit of measure will be written next to the matching fraction. Write that unit of measure in the blank provided.

1. A small bunch of bananas is called what?
.25 _____

47/100 a hank

2. 45 gallons of fresh herring is a what?
.0007 _____

4/100 a bind

3. 560 yards of wool is called a what?
.47 _____

2 75/100 glitches

4. Buttons are measured in units called what?
2.75 _____

1 2/10 a saros

5. 500 pounds of cotton is called a what?
.059 _____

7/100 a billet

7/10000 a pool

6. In England, a 40-inch stick of firewood is called what?
.07 _____

25/100 a hand

7. 6585.32 days are called what by astronomers?
1.2 _____

59/1000 a bale

8. 250 eels are called what?
.04 _____

73

Averages: Whole Numbers

Name_____ Date_____

Not Your Average Track Meet

On your mark . . . get set . . . GO! Our runners are off, hoping to win the gold. But this is no average track meet. Well, actually it *is* an average track meet. These athletes run the race five different times and the one with the best average time wins. Who won today? Find the average time for each runner. Then, put the runners in order from fastest to slowest by writing their names on the spaces at the bottom.

1. Breeze Billings
   Race 1: 45 seconds
   Race 2: 48 seconds
   Race 3: 43 seconds
   Race 4: 45 seconds
   Race 5: 44 seconds
   Average _____

4. Lightnin' Lou
   Race 1: 44 seconds
   Race 2: 47 seconds
   Race 3: 47 seconds
   Race 4: 49 seconds
   Race 5: 43 seconds
   Average _____

2. Fleet Feet Fowler
   Race 1: 40 seconds
   Race 2: 49 seconds
   Race 3: 40 seconds
   Race 4: 40 seconds
   Race 5: 41 seconds
   Average _____

5. Wilma Warpspeed
   Race 1: 45 seconds
   Race 2: 47 seconds
   Race 3: 41 seconds
   Race 4: 41 seconds
   Race 5: 41 seconds
   Average _____

3. Will E. Winn
   Race 1: 46 seconds
   Race 2: 48 seconds
   Race 3: 42 seconds
   Race 4: 42 seconds
   Race 5: 42 seconds
   Average _____

_____ First place

_____ Second place

_____ Third place

_____ Fourth place

_____ Fifth place

On-target Averages

To hit the bull's-eye on this target you need to find the average of each set of numbers. Then find the average of the answers, round it to the nearest hundredth, and write it in the bull's eye. (Use a calculator, if necessary.)

1. 12.12
   40.04
   6.3
   10.01
   _____

2. 2.15
   9.06
   10.29
   59.53
   _____

3. 13.4
   2.6
   11.16
   30.16
   _____

4. 27.3
   21.52
   20.1
   22.222
   _____

Ratios

Name_____ Date_____

Ratio Picnic

It's the year-end school picnic and everyone's invited. And we mean everyone and everything. How can you compare so many different people and things? Using ratios, of course. For each question, look at the picture and count the different items mentioned in the question. Then use these numbers to find the ratio.

What is the ratio of:

1. Bees to flowers? _____
2. Pizza to popsicles? _____
3. Birds to mice? _____
4. Butterflies to nets? _____
5. Sailboats to whales? _____

6. Lakes to trees? _____
7. Dogs to cats? _____
8. Baseballs to bats? _____
9. Frisbees to kites? _____
10. Skateboards to jump ropes? _____

Geometry: Angles

Name _____ Date _____

Raising the Roof With Geometry

These birds have gone building bonkers! Their birdhouses look great, but they all forgot one important thing — to put their roofs on! Please help. It looks like rain! Below each house are the names of the correct roof's angles. Draw a line from each house to the roof that matches the names of the angles found under that house.

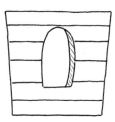

1. one right, two acute

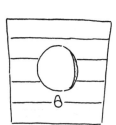

2. two obtuse, two acute

3. four right

a.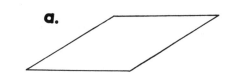

b.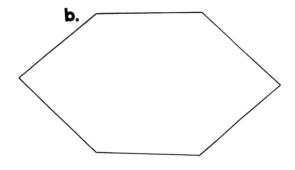

c.

d.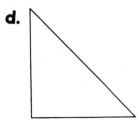

e.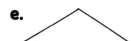

4. one obtuse, two acute

5. four obtuse, two acute

77

Geometry: Shapes

Name_____ Date_____

Shape Sorter

Help! Sam Sorter needs to sort these items according to shape. You can help. Write the name of the shape of each item on the lines provided.

   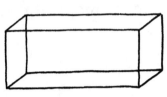

cone   **cube**   **sphere**   **cylinder**   **rectangular prism**

1. dice _____

2. balloon _____

3. can of paint _____

4. cereal box _____

5. planet Mars _____

6. globe _____

7. bowling ball _____

8. funnel _____

9. suitcase _____

10. AA battery _____

11. megaphone _____

12. paper towel roll _____

Measurement: Distance & Conversion

Name_____ Date_____

Fly the Coop

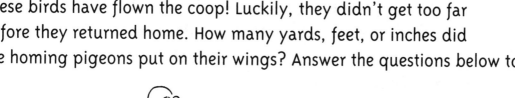

These birds have flown the coop! Luckily, they didn't get too far before they returned home. How many yards, feet, or inches did the homing pigeons put on their wings? Answer the questions below to find out.

How far is that in . . .

1. Flyer flew 150 yards.   feet _____   inches _____

2. Feathers McGee flew 2,100 inches.   feet _____   yards _____

3. Claws flew 36 feet.   inches _____   yards _____

4. Ruthie the Rambler flew 57 yards.   feet _____   inches _____

5. Beatrice Birdbrain flew 126,720 inches.   feet _____   yards _____

6. Wendy Wings flew 80 yards.   feet _____   inches _____

7. Lucy Landingpad flew 243 feet.   yards _____   inches _____

8. Coop Cooper flew 1,800 inches.   feet _____   yards _____

Challenge:

Perry Pigeon flew 2 miles.   feet _____   inches _____

79

Measurement: Area

Name_____ Date_____

The Math Mower

Whew! Our groundskeeper is almost all "mowed" out. And he still has to mow these fields before the games on Saturday. He wants to mow the one with the biggest area first. Give him a hand. Find each field's area. Write your answer in each field.

1.
l = 5 feet   w = 5 feet

2.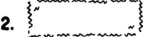
l = 7 feet   w = 2 feet

3.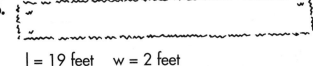
l = 19 feet   w = 2 feet

4.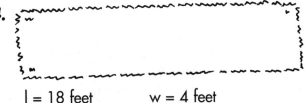
l = 18 feet   w = 4 feet

5.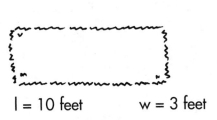
l = 10 feet   w = 3 feet

6.
l = 8 feet   w = 4 feet

7.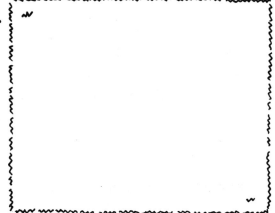
l = 16 feet   w = 13 feet

8.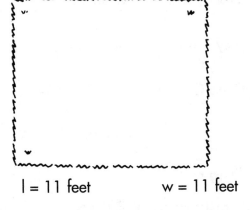
l = 11 feet   w = 11 feet

What is the area of the largest field? _____

Measurement: Volume

Name_____ Date_____

Math Dives Deep

Come on in—the water's fine—or at least it will be once these pools are filled. Find the volume of each pool below to discover how much water each one needs. Write your answer in each pool.

1.  l = 11 ft. w = 12 ft. d = 3 ft.

2.  l = 30 ft. w = 3 ft. d = 3 ft.

3.  l = 20 ft. w = 5 ft. d = 10 ft.

4. l = 40 ft. w = 4 ft. d = 5 ft.

5.  l = 8 ft. w = 8 ft. d = 8 ft.

7.  l = 10 ft. w = 4 ft. d = 10 ft.

6. 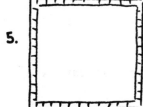 l = 9 ft. w = 7 ft. d = 5 ft.

8.  l = 10 ft. w = 6 ft. d = 4 ft.

Which pool will need the most water? _____

Measurement: Working With Time

Name_____ Date_____

Make "Time" for Math

See how much time it takes you to answer these time questions!

1. Alex has to take two planes to get home. His first flight lasts 1 hour and 38 minutes. His second flight lasts 3 hours and 54 minutes. How much time did he fly altogether, in hours and minutes?

   _____

2. The plane to Los Angeles leaves at 5:50 P.M. The plane to New York leaves 720 seconds later. What time did the plane to New York leave?

   _____

3. The train to Chicago leaves at 2:43 P.M. It arrives 3 hours and 45 minutes later. What time does the train arrive?

   _____

4. DJ Minute Man plays three songs in a row. The first is 3 minutes and 35 seconds long, the second is 4 minutes and 2 seconds long, and the third is 2 minutes and 59 seconds long. What is the total amount of time he has spent playing the three songs?

   _____

5. DJ Minute Man plays a song that's 3 minutes and 40 seconds long. The next song is 50 seconds shorter. How long is the second song?

   _____

6. Mary is cooking dinner. The appetizers take 1 hour and 43 minutes to prepare. The main course takes 2 hours and 24 minutes to prepare. The dessert takes 58 minutes to prepare. How much time has Mary spent cooking?

   _____

Graphing: Coordinate Grid

Name_____ Date_____

Math on the Map

Ready to hit the road? Hope you packed your math skills! That's what you need to read grid maps like the one we have here. Each grid box on the map is labeled with a letter and a number. Use the grid labels to help you answer each question.

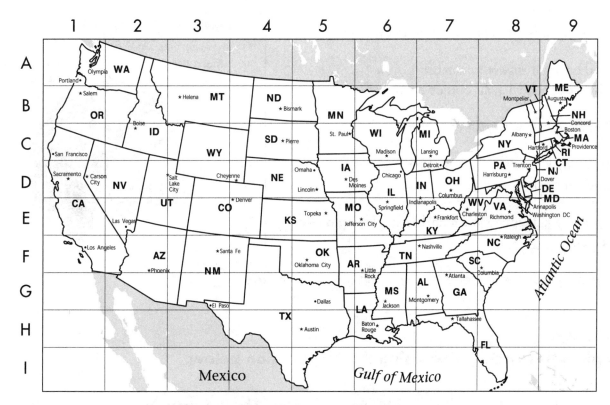

1. Your first stop is a state capital in section C8. Where are you? _____

2. In which section will you find your next stop, Dallas, Texas? _____
   Is all of Texas in the same section? _____

3. Time to go to Los Angeles, California. Which section are you looking for? _____

4. Next stop: Chicago, Illinois. In which section is this city located? _____

5. From Chicago, it's off to I8. Where are you now? _____

6. Get ready for sightseeing in a state capital in F5! Where are you now?
   _____

Challenge:
Now it's time to head home!
Which section is your town in? _____
List all of the sections that your state is in. _____
_____

83

Graphing: Circle Graph

Name _____ Date _____

Graph Attack

Everyone loves to play outside, right? But some kids like it more than others. Look at this graph to see what we mean. Read the graph and answer the questions.

1. How many kids are represented on this graph? _____

2. Based on your answer to number 1, how many kids spend 1 hour outside each day? _____

3. Fill in the graph with your answer to number 2.

4. How many kids spend 1 hour or more playing outside each day? _____

5. How many kids spend less than 1 hour playing outside each day? _____

6. How many kids spend 1 or 2 hours playing outside each day? _____

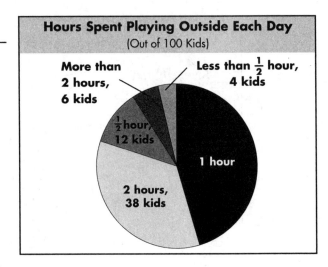

Challenge:
Complete this circle graph using the information below.

- 51 said they surf the World Wide Web.
- 28 said they check and send e-mail.
- 15 said they play computer games.
- 4 said they do homework.
- 2 said they do other things.

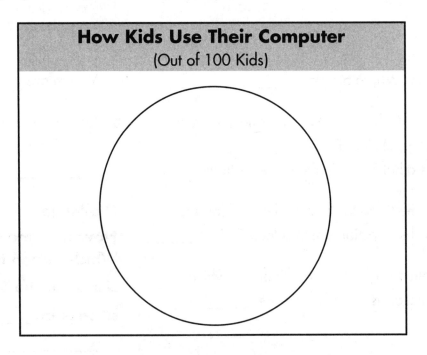

84

Graphing: Line Graph

Name_____ Date_____

Hop on This Number Line

Help these funky frogs find their groovy pads. Read each sentence below. Then write each frog's name on the correct lily pad on the number line. We did one for you. Hop to it!

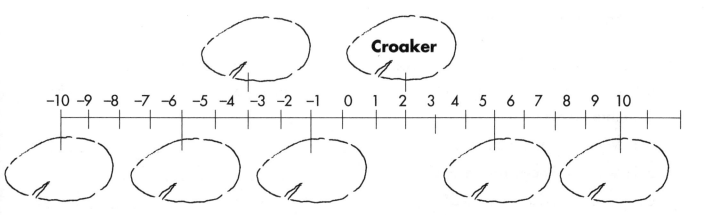

Frank Frog's pad is 3 less than Croaker's.

Philip Frog's pad is 6 more than Frank's.

Filomena Frog's pad is 8 less than Philip's.

Felicity Frog's pad is 4 less than Frank's.

Bully Frog's pad is 4 more than Philip's.

Fillmore Frog's pad is 18 less than Bully's.

85

Word Problems: Mixed Skills

Name_____ Date_____

Putting it All Together

How sharp are your math skills? Answer these questions to find out.

1. Kelly decided to sell her collection of 600 baseball cards. She sold $\frac{1}{4}$ of them the first week. The second week she sold $\frac{2}{5}$ of them. The third week she sold $\frac{1}{3}$ of them.
   a. What fraction of the cards was sold? _____
   b. What fraction of the cards was left? _____

2. The organizers for the annual puppy pound picnic are buying party favors. Each dog will get to take home the following in its doggie bag: 4 old slippers, 3 bones, and 5 fetching sticks. There are 70 dogs at the picnic.
   a. How many bones are needed?_____
   b. How many slippers are needed? _____
   c. How many sticks are needed?_____

3. The school newspaper had a bake sale this week and the members sold cupcakes. They sold 28 cupcakes on Monday, 35 on Tuesday, 38 on Wednesday, 30 on Thursday, and 40 on Friday.
   a. What was the average number of cupcakes sold on one day? _____
   b. If cupcakes were 25 cents each, how much money did the newspaper make?_____

4. Laura babysits for $5 an hour over the weekend. She babysits 2 hours Friday night, 3 hours Saturday, and 1 hour Sunday.
   a. How much money did she earn on Saturday? _____
   b. How many hours did she babysit altogether?_____
   c. How much money did she earn altogether? _____

5. Lisa got $\frac{8}{11}$ of the questions right on the math test. Carol got $\frac{7}{9}$ right on her spelling test. John got $\frac{17}{20}$ right on his social studies quiz.
   a. What fraction did John get wrong?_____
   b. What fraction did Carol get wrong? _____

Answer Key

Page 7
1. 71
2. 145
3. 104
4. 216
5. 84
6. 78
7. 72
8. 141
9. 72
10. 100

The winning submarine is number 2.

Page 8
1. 19
2. 164
3. 66
4. 311
5. 25
6. 24
7. 27
8. 134
9. 189
10. 9
11. 789
12. 89

Player number 11 got the most hits, 789, and he took the most swings.

Page 9
1. 225
2. 31
3. 529
4. 780
5. 110
6. 340
7. 9
8. 509
9. 511
10. 85
11. 277
12. 668
13. 832
14. 334
15. 338

Page 10
29, 7, 17, 5, 11, 3, 19, 13, 23

Page 11
Students should follow the numbers 17, 5, 97, 11, 29, 13, 3, 19 to the nuts.

Page 12
Students should follow the problems 5 x 5, 9 x 3, 7 x 9, and 9 x 5 to the grade book.

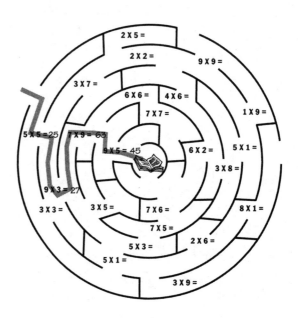

87

Page 13

Students should shade the squares with even numbers. The pet is a RAT.

2 x 4 8	4 x 4 16	2 x 8 10	7 x 1 7	7 x 9 56	6 x 1 6	8 x 7 56	5 x 1 5	2 x 3 6	4 x 9 36	5 x 8 40
4 x 4 16	7 x 3 21	3 x 4 12	5 x 3 15	5 x 2 10	7 x 1 7	4 x 7 28	3 x 7 21	7 x 5 35	4 x 8 32	5 x 9 45
6 x 2 12	5 x 6 30	9 x 1 9	3 x 5 15	5 x 4 20	4 x 5 20	3 x 6 18	5 x 5 25	9 x 5 45	2 x 6 12	5 x 7 35
4 x 3 12	3 x 3 9	2 x 8 16	11 x 5 55	4 x 6 24	11 x 3 33	6 x 3 18	9 x 7 63	3 x 9 27	2 x 7 14	9 x 9 81
3 x 2 6	11 x 7 77	4 x 2 8	1 x 5 5	4 x 1 4	1 x 3 3	2 x 9 18	3 x 1 3	1 x 1 1	3 x 8 24	11 x 9 99

Page 14

1. 24
2. 11
3. 30
4. 32
5. 63
6. 64
7. 27
8. 44
9. 12
10. 42

Page 15

Move the inside ring clockwise 2 places. 86 x 1 = 86, 48 x 2 = 96, 29 x 3 = 87, 56 x 4 = 224, 19 x 7 = 133, 21 x 8 = 168, 13 x 9 = 117, 27 x 5 = 135

Page 16

1. 48
2. 128
3. 180
4. 459
5. 279
6. 126
7. 246
8. 480
9. 639
10. 28
11. 148
12. 156

9 won. 8 came in second.
4 came in third.

Page 17

1. 24 x 1 = 24 (T)
2. 52 x 7 = 364 (H)
3. 68 x 3 = 204 (E)
4. 90 x 6 = 540 (G)
5. 45 x 8 = 360 (R)
6. 88 x 2 = 176 (O)
7. 17 x 9 = 153 (U)
8. 31 x 5 = 155 (N)
9. 76 x 4 = 304 (D)

Riddle answer: THE GROUND

Page 18

1. 156
2. 242
3. 252
4. 156
5. 756
6. 1,577
7. 1,222
8. 576
9. 200
10. 748

Constellation 6 has the most stars.

Page 19

						5	6	2	5			
		3		6	7	2			1	3	8	6
	8	6	4	8		9	8	0	1		4	
2	9	4		0		6			7		7	
	9			4		2			0			

Page 20

1. 962; 1,345; POODLE SKIRT,
2. 936; 812; 574; POUNDCAKE,
3. 973; 824; 615; DOGGONEIT,
4. 894; 763; 1,025; FLEAMARKET

Page 21

Row 1—7,704; 8,954; 9,571; 9,090; 5,988;
Row 2—6,318; 3,638; 9,264; 8,628; 8,822;
Row 3—5,168; 6,930; 7,749; 5,618; 6,710

Page 22
1. 8,901
2. 5,885
3. 5,520
4. 9,312
5. 9,515
6. 32,438
7. 25,500
8. 1,000
9. 33,344

Riddle answer: Germany

Page 23
1. 14,864
2. 7,777
3. 88,642
4. 8,062
5. 3,699
6. 93,666
7. 4,848
8. 9,999

Riddle answer: Because they're always "leaving"!

Page 24
1. 10 ÷ 5 = 2
2. 25 ÷ 5 = 5
3. 20 ÷ 5 = 4
4. 50 ÷ 5 = 10
5. 45 ÷ 5 = 9
6. 55 ÷ 5 = 11
7. 5 ÷ 5 = 1
8. 15 ÷ 5 = 3
9. 35 ÷ 5 = 7
10. 40 ÷ 5 = 8

6 needs the most gloves.

Page 25
1. 9
2. 12
3. 8
4. 7
5. 3
6. 11
7. 1
8. 2
9. 5
10. 10
11. 6
12. 4

Page 26
1. 56 ÷ 8 = 7
2. 144 ÷ 12 = 12
3. 72 ÷ 9 = 8
4. 24 ÷ 6 = 4
5. 60 ÷ 5 = 12
6. 18 ÷ 2 = 9
7. 49 ÷ 7 = 7
8. 120 ÷ 10 = 12
9. 121 ÷ 11 = 11
10. 30 ÷ 3 = 10

The jellyfish in problems 2, 5, and 8 all get the same amount, 12.

Page 27
Students should circle the underlined word or portion of the following words:
si_x_th-grade (54 ÷ 9 = 6)
Five (10 ÷ 2 = 5)
ph_one_ (8 ÷ 8 = 1)
t_one_ (9 ÷ 9 = 1)
eight (72 ÷ 9 = 8),
frigh_ten_ed (60 ÷ 6 = 10)
seven (49 ÷ 7 = 7)
Gel_four_ (12 ÷ 3 = 4)
ca_nine_ (81 ÷ 9 = 9)
tunn_el even_ (77 ÷ 7 = 11)
seven (56 ÷ 8 = 7)
Five (30 ÷ 6 = 5)
atten_tion_ (40 ÷ 4 = 10)
It_ won't_ (8 ÷ 4 = 2)
fr_eight_ (48 ÷ 6 = 8)
Se_th Reeds_ (27 ÷ 9 = 3)

Page 28
1. $3, $4
2. $7, $8
3. $16, $15
4. $6, $5
5. $15, $14
6. $11, $10

Page 29
91; 202; 51; 109; 706; 102; 61; 124; 43; 80;

A LABORATORY RETRIEVER

Page 30
5 r3 (H), 8 r2 (E), 2 r3 (H), 7 r1 (A), 4 r6 (S), 9 r8 (W), 3 r2 (E), 6 r4 (B), 7 r4 (B), 5 r2 (E), 9 r7 (D), 2 r5 (F), 4 r2 (E), 3 r2 (E), 8 r0 (T); He has webbed feet.

Page 31
71 r4 (L), 54 r6 (A), 80 r3 (U), 39 r1 (N), 64 r7 (C), 94 r2 (H), 82 r3 (T), 49 r2 (I), 78 r1 (M), 39 r8 (E); LAUNCH TIME

Page 32
1. 13
2. 15
3. 60
4. 18
5. 24
6. 8
7. 7
8. 21
9. 12
10. 50
11. 39
12. 22

Chef number 3 won with 60 chips were in each cookie.

Page 33

	A	B	C
D	5	2	7
E	1	3	9
F	4	6	8

	A	B	C
D	1	8	2
E	5	6	3
F	7	4	9

Page 34
Row 1: 9, 11, 5, 6
Row 2: 4, 7, 3, 2
Row 3: 8, 15, 13, 12
Row 4: 14, 10, 17, 16

Page 35
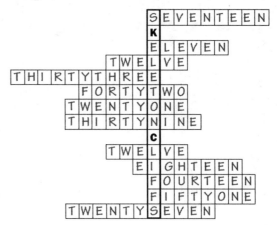

Page 36
1. 320 r16
2. 200 r12
3. 201 r3
4. 100 r8
5. 458 r16
6. 143 r10
7. 1,107 r9
8. 535 r5

Cow number 7 has the farthest to go.

Page 37
819 ÷ 45 = 18 r9,
903 ÷ 33 = 27 r12,
486 ÷ 16 = 30 r6,
619 ÷ 51 = 12 r7,
878 ÷ 58 = 15 r8,
504 ÷ 25 = 20 r4,
483 ÷ 11 = 43 r10

Page 38
1. 52
2. 7,056
3. 46
4. 81
5. 34
6. 259,840
7. 39
8. 1,207
9. 33
10. 352
11. 30
12. 8,991
13. 53
14. 18,980
15. 19

Page 39
1. a. 100 b. 40
2. a. 400 b. 1,000 c. 2,000
3. a. 47 b. 235
4. a. $4.35
5. a. $32.50 b. 2 c. 10 d. 5

Riddle answer: He needed some "dough"!

Page 40
1. a. 381 b. 1,905 c. 508
2. a. 69 b. 92 c. 46
3. a. 60 b. 90 c. 54
4. a. 65 b. 105 c. 143

Page 41
Students should circle the following problems:
714 x 8 (710 x 8 = 5,680),
209 x 6 (210 x 6 = 1,260),
1,119 x 7 (1,100 x 7 = 7,700).

Page 42
90, 40, 60, 50, 80, 20, 70, 700, 900, 400, 800, 600

```
F T L G Q S X C V T I N S S
O O D E R D N U H T H G I E
U M R H M O O I P R X U X V
R Y Z T V B G U N Y D D T E
H O N L Y B V C S E T P Y N
U R Y T H G I E S S T F H T
N I N E H U N D R E D Y I Y
D E R D N U H N E V E S G F
R A K J N C G V T B Q W E T
E A E O T W E N T Y T U O P
D E R D N U H X I S K H J K
```

Page 43
1. a. 400 b. 300 c. 700
2. a. 200 b. 600 c. 800
3. a. 400 b. 900 c. 1,300
4. a. 600 b. 450 c. 1,000
5. briar patch

Page 44
1. $\frac{3}{8}$ 6. $\frac{1}{4}$
2. $\frac{5}{8}$ 7. $\frac{3}{5}$
3. $\frac{1}{6}$ 8. $\frac{2}{5}$
4. $\frac{5}{6}$ 9. $\frac{4}{7}$
5. $\frac{3}{4}$ 10. $\frac{3}{7}$

Page 45

The picture shows a sailboat on the water.

Page 46

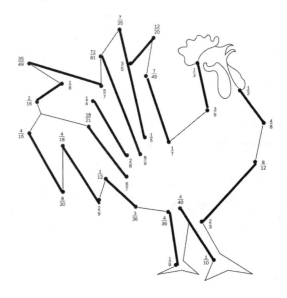

Page 47
Fractions in order from smallest to largest are:

$\frac{1}{3}$ $\frac{1}{2}$ $\frac{3}{5}$ $\frac{5}{8}$ $\frac{4}{6}$ $\frac{3}{4}$
$\frac{7}{9}$ $\frac{9}{10}$

Page 48
Completed cheerleading number line should look like this:

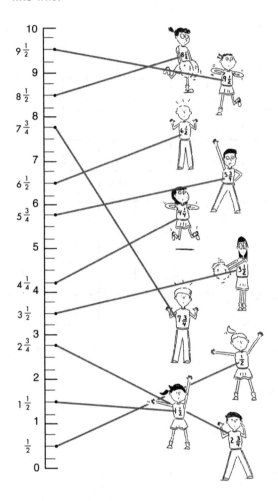

Page 49
fractions equivalent to $\frac{2}{5}$ are

$\frac{20}{50}$ $\frac{10}{25}$ $\frac{18}{45}$ $\frac{24}{60}$ $\frac{4}{10}$ $\frac{6}{15}$ $\frac{8}{20}$ $\frac{22}{55}$

$\frac{26}{65}$ $\frac{28}{70}$ $\frac{30}{75}$ $\frac{32}{80}$ $\frac{200}{500}$ $\frac{40}{100}$ $\frac{80}{200}$

Page 50
$\frac{1}{4} + \frac{3}{4} = 1$ (Cong),

$\frac{2}{6} + \frac{1}{6} = \frac{1}{2}$ (ratulations,),

$\frac{5}{12} + \frac{6}{12} = \frac{11}{12}$ (Cl),

$\frac{3}{8} + \frac{3}{8} = \frac{3}{4}$ (ue! You),

$\frac{1}{9} + \frac{2}{9} = \frac{1}{3}$ (have),

$\frac{4}{15} + \frac{7}{15} = \frac{11}{15}$ (pieced),

$\frac{1}{7} + \frac{5}{7} = \frac{6}{7}$ (together),

$\frac{2}{17} + \frac{8}{17} = \frac{10}{17}$ (your),

$\frac{1}{8} + \frac{1}{8} = \frac{1}{4}$ (first),

$\frac{1}{5} + \frac{2}{5} = $ (mystery),

Congratulations, Clue! You have pieced together your first mystery!

Page 51
1. c
2. b
3. a
4. a

Page 52
$\frac{1}{2} + \frac{1}{3} = \frac{5}{6}$ (H), $\frac{1}{4} + \frac{2}{8} = \frac{1}{2}$ (I), $\frac{5}{9} + \frac{1}{3} = \frac{8}{9}$ (T),

$\frac{5}{12} + \frac{1}{6} = \frac{7}{12}$ (O), $\frac{1}{7} + \frac{1}{21} = \frac{4}{21}$ (M), $\frac{1}{12} + \frac{1}{3} = \frac{5}{12}$ (F),

$\frac{1}{10} + \frac{2}{5} = \frac{1}{2}$ (I), $\frac{1}{3} + \frac{1}{9} = \frac{4}{9}$ (X), $\frac{1}{3} + \frac{1}{6} = \frac{1}{2}$ (I),

$\frac{3}{4} + \frac{1}{8} = \frac{7}{8}$ (N), $\frac{1}{11} + \frac{3}{11} = \frac{4}{11}$ (G), $\frac{2}{15} + \frac{2}{3} = \frac{4}{5}$ (L),

$\frac{2}{12} + \frac{5}{12} = \frac{7}{12}$ (O), $\frac{7}{20} + \frac{2}{5} = \frac{3}{4}$ (C), $\frac{1}{4} + \frac{3}{8} = \frac{5}{8}$ (K),

$\frac{1}{14} + \frac{5}{7} = \frac{11}{14}$ (A), $\frac{7}{9} + \frac{1}{9} = \frac{8}{9}$ (T), $\frac{2}{3} + \frac{2}{9} = \frac{8}{9}$ (T),

$\frac{2}{12} + \frac{2}{6} = \frac{1}{2}$ (I), $\frac{1}{2} + \frac{1}{4} = \frac{3}{4}$ (C),

HI TOM, I'm home from work early, I am FIXING the broken LOCK on the door in the ATTIC!

Page 53
BULLFROG

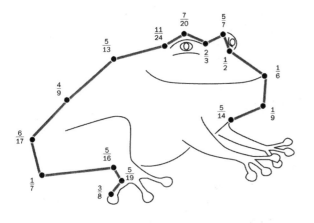

Page 54

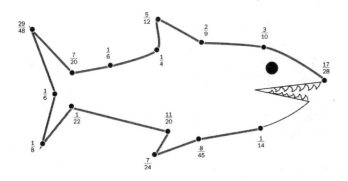

Page 55
Conveyor belt number 1:
Students should show all their work; 5

1. $\frac{1}{2}$
2. $\frac{5}{6}$
3. $\frac{21}{44}$
4. $\frac{3}{5}$
5. $\frac{3}{12}$

Page 56
ELEPHANT

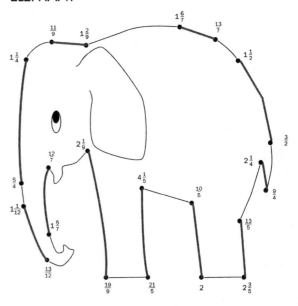

Page 57

$\frac{89}{8} = 11\frac{1}{8}$ $\frac{10}{3} = 3\frac{1}{3}$ $\frac{3}{2} = 1\frac{1}{2}$

$\frac{79}{12} = 6\frac{7}{12}$ $\frac{19}{5} = 3\frac{4}{5}$ $\frac{68}{9} = 7\frac{5}{9}$

$\frac{9}{8} = 1\frac{1}{8}$ $\frac{36}{5} = 7\frac{1}{5}$ $\frac{7}{2} = 3\frac{1}{2}$

$\frac{16}{11} = 1\frac{5}{11}$ $\frac{37}{4} = 9\frac{1}{4}$ $\frac{7}{4} = 1\frac{3}{4}$

Shaded picture shows a catfish.

Page 58
1. 1.77
2. 9.44
3. 6.76
4. 8.70
5. 6.05
6. 12.56
7. 3.09
8. 0.15
9. 24.99
10. 3.90

Page 59
255–1337

Page 60
3.1 (SE), 3.11 (C), 3.25 (RE), 3.92 (T), 4.0 (OF), 4.09 (T), 4.9 (HE), 5.14 (J), 5.2 (EW), 5.51 (E), 5.9 (L), 6.03 (T), 6.3 (H), 6.31 (I), 6.39 (E), 6.48 (F), 7.07 (BY), 7.09 (I), 7.11 (O), 7.21 (N), 7.26 (A), 7.41 (J), 7.45 (E), 7.47 (T);

SECRET OF THE JEWEL THIEF BY IONA JET

Page 61
Audition Schedule
12:45:   .0900
1 o'clock: .90
1:15:   1.01
1:30:   2.01
1:45:   2.10
2 o'clock: 2.11
2:15:   3.59
2:30:   3.97
2:45:   4.6900
3 o'clock: 4.70

Page 62
The decimals rounded to the nearest whole number are:

Row 1—115, 120, (136), 118
Row 2—158, 150, 141, 151
Row 3—138, 133, 135, (136)
Row 4—125, 140, 157, 116

Page 63
Path 1—$82.02
Path 2—$91.48
Path 3—$79.30
Path 4—$66.12
Path 2 contains the most gold

Page 64
Row 1: 92.7, 26, (222.2)
Row 2: 199.6, 61.6, 227.1
Row 3: 109, 298.6, (222.2)

Page 65
Across—A. 1.97, E. 38.72, F. 3.96, H. 4.8, I. 7.9;
Down—B. 9.8, C. 123, D. 5.9, G. 6.78, H. 49.6

Page 66
From least to greatest the answers are 38, 69.5, 114, 185.6, 241.3, 258.9, 267.2, 280.1, 311.8

Page 67
Heather
$99 - $18.99 = 80.01
80.01 - 18.99 = 61.02
61.02 - 18.99 = 42.03
42.03 - 18.99 = 23.04
23.04 - 18.99 = 4.05
Heather has $4.05 left over.

Lisa
$99 - $19.99 = 79.01
79.01 - 19.99 = 59.02
59.02 - 19.99 = 39.03
39.03 - 19.99 = 19.04
Lisa has $19.04 left over.

Jack
$99 - $20.99 = 78.01
78.01 - 20.99 = 57.02
57.02 - 20.99 = 36.03
36.03 - 20.99 = 15.04
Jack has $15.04 left over.

Lisa has the most money left over.
Heather spent the most.

Page 68
Shopper Number 1 spent $19.45 and has $30.55 left over.
Shopper Number 2 spent $20.55 and has $29.45 left over.

Answers will vary, but students should explain their method clearly.

Page 69
Across—A. $36.57, B. $44.55, D. $6.60, E. $7.12, G. $161.91, I $7.52, K. $78.72;
Down—A. $35.05, B. $56.70, C. $43.61, F. $2.31, H. $6.72, J. $2.50

Page 70
black leather gloves: 3 x $6.99 = $20.97
work gloves: $10.27 x 6 = $61.62
sandals: 4 x $7.89 = $31.56
plastic gloves: 10 x $1.00 = $10.00

Page 71
Mandy (jacket and skirt) 1.3 x 12.8 = 16.64
Sandy (sweater and shorts) 21.6 x 2.6 = 56.16
Candy (blazer and pants) 9.7 x 6.7 = 64.99
Brandy (dress and hat) 38.1 x 1.4 = 53.34

Page 72
1. 5.082
2. 2
3. 3.9996
4. 22
5. 15.96
6. 1,010
7. 525
8. 17.5
9. 18.12

Riddle answer: Get to the "point"!

Page 73
1. $\frac{25}{100}$ a hand
2. $\frac{7}{10000}$ a pool
3. $\frac{47}{100}$ a hank
4. $2\frac{75}{100}$ glitches
5. $\frac{59}{1000}$ a bale
6. $\frac{7}{100}$ a billet
7. $1\frac{2}{10}$ a saros
8. $\frac{4}{100}$ a bind

Page 74
1. 45 seconds
2. 42 seconds
3. 44 seconds
4. 46 seconds
5. 43 seconds

Correct finishing order is: Fleet Feet, Wilma, Will E., Breeze, and Lou.

Page 75
1. 17.1175
2. 20.2575
3. 14.33
4. 16.7105
Bull's Eye: 17.10

Page 76
1. 3:4
2. 5:2
3. 4:1
4. 7:3
5. 5:1
6. 1:1
7. 5:6
8. 5:4
9. 2:1
10. 2:4

Page 77
1. d
2. a
3. c
4. e
5. b

Page 78
1. cube
2. sphere
3. cylinder
4. rectangular prism
5. sphere
6. sphere
7. sphere
8. cone
9. rectangular prism
10. cylinder
11. cone
12. cylinder

Page 79
1. 450 feet; 5,400 inches
2. 175 feet; 58 1/3 yards
3. 432 inches; 12 yards
4. 171 feet; 2,052 inches
5. 10,560 feet; 3,520 yards
6. 240 feet; 2,880 inches
7. 81 yards; 2,916 inches
8. 150 feet; 50 yards

Challenge: 10,560 feet; 3,520 yards

Page 80
1. 25 sq. ft.
2. 14 sq. ft.
3. 38 sq. ft.
4. 72 sq. ft.
5. 30 sq. ft.
6. 32 sq. ft.
7. 208 sq. ft.
8. 121 sq. ft.

The largest field is number 7.

Page 81
1. 396 cu. ft.
2. 270 cu. ft.
3. 1,000 cu. ft.
4. 800 cu. ft.
5. 512 cu. ft.
6. 315 cu. ft.
7. 400 cu. ft.
8. 240 cu. ft.

Pool number 3 contains the most water.

Page 82
1. 5 hours, 32 minutes
2. 6:02 PM
3. 6:28 PM
4. 10 minutes, 36 seconds
5. 2 minutes, 50 seconds
6. 5 hours, 5 minutes

Page 83
1. Albany, NY
2. G5, No
3. F1
4. D6
5. Florida
6. Oklahoma City, OK
7. Answers will vary.

Page 84
1. 100
2. 40
3. Students should write in 40 next to the section labeled 1 hour.
4. 84
5. 16
6. 78

Challenge: Check that students have filled in the appropriate section with the correct number and labeled their graph clearly.

Page 85
Frank Frog's pad is at -2.
Phillip Frog's pad is at 4.
Filomena Frog's pad is at -4.
Felicity Frog's pad is at -6.
Bully Frog's pad is at 8.
Fillmore Frog's pad is at -10.

Page 86
1. a. 59/60 b. 1/60
2. a. 210 b. 280 c. 350
3. a. 34.2 b. $42.75
5. a. $15 b. 6 hours c. $30
6. a. 3/20 b. 2/9